W9-BRK-684

CONCILIUM

Religion in the Seventies

CONCILIUM
Religion in the Seventies

EDITORIAL DIRECTORS: Edward Schillebeeckx (Dogma) •
Herman Schmidt (Liturgy) • Alois Müller (Pastoral) •
Hans Küng (Ecumenism) • Franz Böckle (Moral Theology) •
Johannes B. Metz (Church and World) • Roger Aubert (Church
History) • Teodoro Jiménez Urresti (Canon Law) • Christian
Duquoc (Spirituality) • Pierre Benoît and Roland Murphy
(Scripture)

CONSULTING EDITORS: Marie-Dominique Chenu • ✠Carlo
Colombo • Yves Congar • Andrew Greeley • Jorge Mejía •
Karl Rahner • Roberto Tucci

EXECUTIVE SECRETARY: (Awaiting new appointment),
Arksteestraat 3–5, Nijmegen, The Netherlands

Volume 72: Liturgy

EDITORIAL BOARD: Herman Schmidt • David Power •
Jan van Cauwelaert • Irénée-Henry Dalmais • Luigi Della Torre •
Balthasar Fischer • Adalberto Franquesa • Joseph Gelineau •
Mgr Denis Hurley • Joseph Jungmann • Aidan Kavanagh •
Emil Lengeling • Juan Llopis • Gerard Lukken •
Thierry Maertens • Luis Maldonado • Hendrick Manders •
Salvatore Marsili • Josef Martín Patino • Juan Mateos •
Frederick McManus • Jairo Mejía Gomez • Placid Murray •
Franz Nikolasch • Ignacio Oñatibia • Joseph Pascher •
Jordi Pinell Pons • Heinrich Rennings • Juan Rivera Recio •
Philippe Rouillard • Alfredo Trusso • Cipriano Vagaggini •
Cyrille Vogel • Mgr. Guilford Young

LITURGY

SELF-EXPRESSION
OF THE CHURCH

Volume 72

Edited by

Herman Schmidt, S.J.

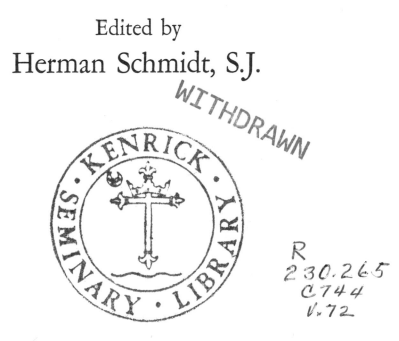

WITHDRAWN

KENRICK SEMINARY LIBRARY

R
230.265
C744
V.72

Herder and Herder

721553

1972
HERDER AND HERDER NEW YORK
232 Madison Avenue, New York 10016

Cum approbatione Ecclesiastica

Library of Congress Catalog Card Number: 77–168650
Copyright © 1972 by Herder and Herder, Inc. and Stichting Concilium.
All rights reserved. Nothing contained in this publication shall be reproduced
and/or made public by means of print, photographic print, microfilm, or in
any other manner without the previous consent of the Stichting Concilium
and the publishers.

Printed in the United States

CONTENTS

PART III
DOCUMENTATION CONCILIUM

Editorial

AS liturgy is the expression in worship of the Church as God's
people, it has a profound effect on the Church as communion and
mission. Ecclesiology stresses the nature of the Church as *diakonia*
and the many services which contribute to its life and mission.
This vitality of the Church must receive due expression in worship, and in this issue of *Concilium* we are concerned with the
subject of liturgical ministry. This is an important topic for the
renewal of the liturgy and of the Church itself, since "the work
of the whole people of God, structured in its variety of orders
and ministries, should be visible in the way the reform is carried
out" (*Third Instruction for the Correct Implementation of the
Constitution on the Sacred Liturgy*, 5 September 1970).

From an historical perspective, the first article notes the alienation between official cult and Christian community. This is in
large part due to the concept of priestly ministry incorporated
into worship, and to the practical suppression of all community
ministries other than those of the bishop and the ordained priest.
The second article endeavours to outline a theological perspective;
and the other articles take up different aspects of liturgical ministry as these are currently relevant. Obviously we are not exclusively, or even primarily, concerned with the ministry of the
ordained priest, but we wished the treatment of the question to
be as broad as possible.

None the less, not every aspect is treated, since it is not possible
to cover everything in a single issue and it is not always easy
to realize a plan exactly as it was envisaged at the start. Some

discussion about the factual and sociological basis for the gathering in worship of a community of people would have been desirable. This involves the ecclesiological question of the nature of the local church, but it also touches on the liturgical ministry because it raises the problem of the appropriate criteria to be used in the choice of liturgical ministers, including the ordained president.

We would also have liked some treatment of assemblies which gather without the presidency of an ordained minister. This is not to suggest that there can be a celebration of the Eucharist (or indeed of the other sacraments) without an ordained priest, yet there are other prayer services and celebrations which do not require this presidency but still need their ministers.

The instruction on the liturgy quoted above is in fact very much concerned about the hierarchical control of liturgy and its reform. The modalities of such control are open to debate, since it must harmonize with the principle that the liturgy is the work of the people of God. There is an obvious tension between the desire for greater freedom in the exercise of the liturgy and the desire to submit it to strict hierarchical control. Hence the bulletin on worship in a free assembly. The first two contributions give examples of what occurs in free assemblies of one sort or another. The third discusses the principles involved and underlines the factors inherent in the current malaise. In line with this bulletin, the documentation provides examples of how national hierarchies have approached the question of liturgical legislation.

The liturgy is often the place where broader conflicts make themselves felt. The ministries accredited to the assembly, the criteria used in appointing people to their exercise, and the extent of the responsibility afforded them are all reflections of broader issues which lie beneath many of the tensions at work in the life of the Church at present. This is why the subject treated in this issue is important.

DAVID POWER
HERMAN SCHMIDT
HELMUT HUCKE

PART I
ARTICLES

Cyrille Vogel

An Alienated Liturgy

IF THE liturgical historian momentarily abandons his concern for documents (ordinals, sacramentaries, pontificals, and so on) and the bare institutions of the cult, in order to try to appreciate the part played by liturgical activities in the spiritual life of the Christian community, he is forced to acknowledge a serious lack: divine worship is evidently inconsistent with Christian life; it is alienated from the community. Liturgy, which ought not to be anything other than the authentic expression of the community (lest it deny its very nature), has gradually been detached from the community throughout the centuries. In fact, the decline has gone so far as to have produced, in answer to the frustration of religious feeling, a whole ensemble of paraliturgical practices flanking the official liturgy and even deputizing for it. But all these mediocre substitutes really go to prove that the community has *had* to seek for an authentic means of expression. Examples of the kind of thing I mean are the multifarious devotions to the Blessed Sacrament or to the saints.[1] Only in the last few decades has there been any effort made, not to restore the liturgy to its proper place (it is not just an activity—not even one enjoying

---

[1] Such devotions and paraliturgical developments appeared during the third period (from Gregory VII, 1073-85, to the Council of Trent, 1545), and the fourth period (from the Council of Trent to Vatican II) of the history of Christian worship. On the growth of devotion to the Blessed Sacrament, see P. P. Brone, *Die Verehrung der Eucharistie im Mittelalter* (Munich, 1933); for the development of the cult of the saints, see T. Klauser, *Kleine abendländische Liturgiegeschichte* (Bonn, 1965), pp. 100, 125-30.

primacy among all others), but to give back to it its own fundamental authenticity.

The progressive alienation of liturgy from the community has
been recognized not primarily by professional historians but by
those engaged in pastoral practice.[2] Obviously one has to try to
find the cause (or causes) of the process. I shall restrict myself
here to three forms of cultic activity which have been alienated
from community life throughout the centuries—even though this
alienation is not always immediately apparent: (1) The Eucharist,
which lost its status as the major sacred meal and became the
mere *missa privata*; (2) penance, which lost its community function and became private confession; (3) Holy Orders, which lost
their significance as ministry, and were clericalized in an "absolute" form.[3]

However, before considering the forms of alienation under
discussion, some attention must be given to one of their initial
suasions: liturgical language.

I. LITURGICAL LANGUAGE

Because it avoided any linguistic adaptation when the national
languages came into being, liturgy became alien to the general
as well as the religious sensibility of Christian men and women.
It is not necessary to give a detailed account of the close relations
that obtain between a language and the individual or the group:
the basic point is that it *matters* if you have to pray in a language
you can't understand.

The Western Church underwent only two linguistic revolu-
tions in the course of its history: one at the end of the fourth
century, and the other during Vatican II (Constitution on the
Liturgy, 4 December 1963).[4] The transition from the use of Greek

[2] Cf. P.-A. Chassagneux: "Certainly there have been reforms . . . but they
are too insignificant to count" (*Le Monde*, 14 April 1971, p. 19); and the
Bishop of Rheims, Mgr Maury, in the diocesan bulletin, *Reins-Ardennes*,
of 26 March 1971, on the "liturgy of the rich".

[3] For reasons of space, I restrict my remarks to the West. The East,
though to a lesser degree, has undergone a similar process of alienation.

[4] On the problem of languages in the Church, see the basic account by
T. Klauser, "Der übergang der römischen Kirche von der griechischen zur
lateinischen Liturgiesprache", in *Miscellanea G. Mercati*, i (*Studi e Testi*,
121) (Rome, 1946), pp. 147–82; C. Mohrmann, "Les origines de la latinité à
Rome", in *Vigiliae Christianae*, iii (1949), pp. 67–106; 162–82.

to that of Latin in the liturgy took place between 360 and 380; that is to say, it was about a century behind the official language of the Roman community, which was Latinized in about 250. The only communities which used Latin as a basic means of expression from the start were those of North Africa: Tertullian and Cyprian forged the theological, juridical and liturgical language of the Church in the West. All the evidence goes to show that the transition from Greek to Latin did not come about through translations of the Latin texts, but by the *creation* of a new formulary.

No linguistic change intervened for one thousand six hundred years, during the period when the European official languages or vernaculars were formed. This means that throughout all this vast stretch of time the liturgy was really accessible only to the clergy. It was incomprehensible to the faithful and increasingly burdened with arbitrary and complicated rites and a for the most part esoteric symbolism; in addition, it was over-stylized to the point of becoming a mere collection of rubrics. Quite clearly, Christian worship remained alien to the Christian community—and often to those among the clergy who were not professional liturgists or archaeologists. Hence the appearance of extra-liturgical "devotions", and of a para-liturgy that believers could understand.

The refusal to make liturgical formularies accessible by putting them into a tongue understood by the people, and, more generally, to make the sacred action itself comprehensible to all, is not to be attributed solely to liturgical conservatism.

At the height of the Middle Ages, the notion appeared that documents intended for liturgical use and public prayer (the Eucharist, the sacraments, various blessings) were texts reserved *for the exclusive use* of the liturgist and the priestly hierarchy. The ceremonial rubrics tended to restrict not only translation but diffusion and study. A letter from Paris de Grassis to Leo X (11 March 1516) is revealing on this point:

"First of all I shall answer those who believe that religious ceremonies should be made accessible to all men. . . . Your Holiness is well aware that the authority and prestige of the Holy See depend on the attitude of princes and the powerful. They, in fact, believe that Popes are not mortal men but something like gods on earth; they submit to them, obey them, venerate, and even worship them; their admiration is ungrudging when they observe the ceremonies of canonization, imperial coronation, royal anointing, creation of cardinals, consecration of patriarchs, archbishops and bishops, and any other ceremony which seems to have a whiff of the divine about it. But if the secrets of the cult were revealed and ceremonies were made accessible [to all], the immediate result would be a loss of prestige."[5]

One couldn't put it better—that is, in a more naïvely cynical manner. The liturgy had become an esoteric and magical ceremonial intended to foster the power of the hierarchy.

It is proper to recall, in the same context, that Joseph de Voisin's translation (1660) of the Roman Missal was put on the Index; that Alexander VII's *Ad aures nostras* of 12 January 1661 forbade the translation of the Missal—even for private reading among the faithful; that the Bull *Unigenitus* (Clement IX) of 8 September 1713 rejected Quesnel's eighty-sixth proposition (Quesnel: "To deprive the common people of the consolation of combining their own prayers with those of the whole Church is a usage repugnant to the practice of the Apostles and to the designs of God"); and that Pius VI, on 28 August 1794, condemned article 55 of the Synod of Pistoia (Pius VI: "The use of the vernacular in liturgical prayers is false and foolhardy ...").[6]

II. FROM THE EUCHARIST TO THE PRIVATE MASS

The Eucharist is not necessarily "private" if it is celebrated outside a church, in a private residence, or in some temporary location, on condition that a specific—even limited—group of the faithful participate.[7] No more is the Mass "private" when celebrated by a group gathered together for a specific purpose (a funeral, a marriage, and so on), or with a reduced ceremonial.

The mass becomes a private mass when there is only one celebrant and it has no direct connection with an actual, present community, and does not directly serve any pastoral need. It was

[5] Paris de Grassis, *Contra electum Corcyrensem* (Cristoforo Marcello), in Mabillon, *Museum Italicum*, 11 (Paris, 1689), pp. 588–9, 592.

[6] All these documents are given, in chronological order, in Denzinger-Schönmetzer, *Enchiridion symbolorum*, 33 (Freiburg, 1965).

[7] J. Wagner, *Altchristliche Eucharistiefeiern im kleinen Kreis* (unpublished dissertation; Bonn, 1949).

in this precise sense that the private mass appeared in the sixth and seventh centuries, and became widely diffused in the eighth century. More exactly, the *missa privata* came into existence in the monasteries where, from the period mentioned onward, the numbers of ordained monks (who used the celebration of the Eucharist as a form of private devotion[8]) began to increase.

This kind of perversion of the Eucharist—which is properly the most solemn and authentic communal expression of commemoration of the Lord—into a pious devotion, and the sole prerogative of the celebrant priest (whether a monk or not), is surely evidence of a profound deterioration in religious sensibility.[9] A few though adequate indications enable us to grasp the reasons for this deformation, which is not derivable from any historical event or official regulation. The essential cause was a change of theological and ecclesial attitude.

In the primitive Church, the eucharistic celebration was conceivable only in terms of the concelebration of all the community —priests or laymen. This, the oldest understanding of worship, was reinforced by the notion of mystery. From the seventh century onwards, as far as the Germanic and Celtic mentalities were concerned, the emphasis was placed instead on the private individual, to the disadvantage of the community—a process which extended to all spheres of human activity. A kind of "degeneration of mystery" came about. The worshipping society (identical with the community) tended to consider divine service as a collection of practices intended for the *salvation of the individual*. It seemed proper in this perspective, to multiply the number of acts of worship, especially since they took effect automatically.[10]

[8] O. Nussbaum, "Kloster, Priestermönch und Privatmesse", *Theophaneia*, 14 (Bonn, 1961).

[9] The change is clear, too, from the fact that before the seventh century there was an actual *fear* of the celebration of the Eucharist (cf. P. Martin de Braga, *Verba seniorum*, 33, 3; *PL*, 73, 1052), whereas after that period one meets with high praise for those who celebrate private masses every day.

[10] Cf. J. Döring: "The *mysterium* tends towards the *officium quotidianum*" (*Die Privatmesse. Ein Versuch zur Soziologie der frühmittelalterlichen Liturgik* [Dissertation; Marburg, 1925], p. 40, cited in Nussbaum, *op. cit.*, p. 171). The change at the level of eucharistic worship accords with that in the conception of grace. See W. Roetzer, *Des heiligen Augustinus Schriften als Liturgiegeschichtliche Quellen* (Munich, 1930), p. 95; also M. Schmaus, *Katholische Dogmatik*, 3, 2 (1956), pp. 287, 294, *et seq.* The Augustinian

The fear for salvation, encouraged above all in South Gaul by the Pelagian controversies, brought in its train an anxious pursuit of an increasingly "abundant" grace. The idea developed that the most effective means of obtaining these *graces* (the singular was increasingly abandoned in favour of the plural) was the mass. This opinion was probably expressed for the first time by St Isidore of Seville († 633), whose sacramental theory was fundamental to the medieval understanding of the Eucharist.[11] This provided the theological basis for the proliferation of masses. In the ninth century, by the same process of inference, the salvific value of the precious eucharistic blood was frequently asserted.[12] The generally accepted belief was that personal salvation was best assured by the celebration of an optimal number of masses. The Eucharist became the isolated object of private devotion, and eucharistic worship was detached from the community; just as the Christian—in terms of worship—dissociated himself from the community.[13] Votive masses for individuals or for the most diverse individual needs multiplied.[14] By founding chantries, the donor-investor tried to ensure that masses would be said "for the good of his soul" even beyond the grave.[15] The growing number of

doctrine of grace, in contrast to the ascetic mentality which supposed that *missa = opus bonum*, did not receive much support in the Middle Ages, in liturgy or in dogmatic theology.

[11] Cf. the travesty of the definition of the Eucharist propounded by Isidore, *Etymologiae*, 6, 19, 38: "Panis et calicis sacramentum graeci Eucharistiam dicunt, quod latine 'bona gratia [gift from heaven]' interpretatur." On Isidore's influence on eucharistic doctrine, see J. R. Geiselmann, *Die Abendmahlslehre an der Wende der christlichen Spätantike zum Frühmittelalter* (Munich, 1933), pp. 178-230.

[12] Documentation in J. R. Geiselmann, "Die Eucharistielehre der Vorscholastik", *Forschungen z. christl. Litt. u. Dogmengeschichte*, 15 (1926), p. 133.

[13] See A. L. Mayer, "Die Liturgie und der Geist der Gothik", *Jahrbuch f. Liturgiewissenschaft*, 6 (1926), pp. 92-3.

[14] The liturgical version of this phenomenon was that votive masses made up the major part of the *Supplement* which the liturgists at Charlemagne's court provided for the Roman *Hadrianum*.

[15] Chronicle of the monastery of St Bartholomew of Carpineto, 3 (twelfth century): "Tunc ... abbas pro anima praedicti fratris Tasconis *mille missas* Deo facere ... promisit." This was also the reason for the appearance of special fraternities to say mass for their members. See Nussbaum, *op. cit.*, pp. 162-8.

votive masses was rivalled by the "penitential" masses, said to be equivalent to—or even substitutable for—works of mortification.[16]

This striving for the greatest possible number of masses led to an increase in the number of priests concerned solely with saying mass (often several in the one day), and in particular to a proliferation of ordained monks, since the clergy engaged in parish work were obviously too few for the task. To be a priest now meant not so much being in the service of the people of God, as personal sanctification by celebrating the mass—an activity which gradually became the only role proper to the presbyter during the one thousand five hundred years under discussion here.

The main consequence of all this was not only a dissociation of the isolated celebrant from the local community—which became a decisive break with the appearance of the private mass—but a gulf between the celebrant and the applicants for masses. Even though Amalarius of Metz († c. 850) still took it for granted that the applicants would be present at the celebration, this requirement was relaxed later.[17] With that, the alienation of the Eucharist from the community was complete.

A known *economic* consequence of the multiplication of private masses was the enrichment of the monasteries through the gifts supplied by the faithful "in return for" the masses offered.[18]

The consequences for worship were twofold. In the first place, the creation of the plenary missal, the first examples of which appeared in the eighth century (the "Bobbio Missal" at the beginning of the eighth century, according to Dold; and in the seventh, according to Willmart), and which certainly multiplied during the tenth century parallel to the increased celebration of private masses. This development required the celebrant to recite all the prayers and readings, even in the very rare cases of communal celebration. This obligation was in force from 1150 on,

[16] Cf. C. Vogel, "Composition légale et commutations dans le système de la pénitence tarifée", in *Revue de Droit canonique*, 8 (1958), pp. 289–318; 9 (1959), pp. 1–38; 341–59 (esp. p. 30).

[17] The liturgical equivalent of this isolation of the celebrant was that the so-called *prex sacerdotalis* anaphora of Innocent I became in the Middle Ages the *prex mystica* (Isidore, *Etymol.*, 6) or *oratio periculosa* (Roman Penitential, ps. 77).

[18] The first scales of fees belong to this period, cf. C. Vogel, *art. cit.*, pp. 31 and 28–34 (enrichment of the monasteries).

and became general towards the middle of the thirteenth century: it was, in fact, the ritual expression of the break between the Eucharist and the community.[19]

The second ritual consequence was the proliferation of altars in the places where mass was celebrated; the first testimonies to this process are found in the sixth century. (The "seven altars" of the Lateran are seven offertory tables, and not altars!) This proliferation had as a result the fact that, until a relatively recent date, and for topographical reasons, places of worship could not be used for truly communal celebrations. Even when various sub-groups from among the Christian community came together to "assist" at mass, often at the same time and in the same church, the activities in which they participated were—and could be—no more than private masses. There is no point in stressing the almost exclusive emphasis on the elevation, and on the cult of the eucharistic monstrance (which resulted from the desire to "see the Host"), or in dwelling on the sometimes grotesque and always distressing results of this state of affairs.[20]

III. From Ministry to Absolute Ordination

The Christian community is not made up of clergy on the one hand and laymen on the other—if by that one is to understand clergy and laity as representing autonomous states, independent of one another and able to come together in communal activities only on terms which safeguard the fundamental autonomy of each "estate". Neither laity nor clergy by themselves can constitute a local church. The clergy (bishop, presbyter, deacon) have meaning and reality only by virtue of their rootedness in the community as ministers of the word and of sacramental life.

Although the Church was not established as a federation, it developed historically from the *local* community to the supra-local Church—and not vice versa. It is possible to trace the course of how and why the local communities, from the fourth century onwards, regrouped into larger aggregates at the level of the

[19] See Nussbaum, *op. cit.*, pp. 185–203.
[20] On the desire to see the Host, see E. Dumoutet, *Le désir de voir l'hostie et les origines de la dévotion au Saint-Sacrement* (Paris, 1926).

province and the civil diocese (containing several provinces).[21] Just as the clergy in the local community have meaning only by virtue of their sacred function, so in the larger aggregates the clergy "exist" only in so far as they exercise an exactly defined ministry: the bishop at the head of a local church (the metropolitan and patriarch at the level of the province or the diocese); the presbyter in the service of an urban or rural church, or attached to a shrine or a monastic church.

If the ordained man is not appointed to a specific office of service in the community, ordination (even when carried out according to the prescribed rules and rites) is null and void (not only illicit or annulable); this is the ordination which our texts call "absolute", in the sense of being without any ministerial reference.[22] An ordination conferred without any precise pastoral mission, or upon the individual as such, is unreal.

All the available evidence agrees that this was doctrine and practice until approximately the end of the twelfth century. Since that time, but *only since then* (and for reasons that I cannot go into here), any ordination, provided that it is carried out in accordance with the rites as set forth in the official liturgical books, remains valid, even if it is absolute and conferred outside any consistent community.[23]

This change at the end of the twelfth century had as its major consequence a complete uprooting and dissociation of the clergy from the Church.

It will suffice if I cite a few primary texts in this regard. The ecumenical council of Chalcedon (451), c. 6, stipulates: "No one may be ordained in an absolute manner (without connection), whether presbyter, deacon, or cleric of any kind, if he is not

[21] See J. Gaudemet, *L'Eglise dans l'empire romain* (fourth and fifth centuries); *Histoire du Droit et des Institutions de l'Eglise en Occident*, III (Paris, 1958), and the symposium *L'Episcopat et l'Eglise universelle* (*Unum Sanctam*, 39, Paris, 1964).

[22] See V. Fuchs, *Der Ordinationstitel von seiner Entstehung bis auf, Innocenz III* (*Kan. Studien u. Texte*, 4, Bonn, 1930); E. Sohm, *Kirchenrecht*, II, pp. 284-308. On the primitive period, see A. Lemaire, *Les ministères aux origines de l'Eglise* (*Lectio divina*, 68, Paris, 1971).

[23] The doctrine in force in the Western Catholic Church (and only in this Church) from the end of the twelfth century reinforced the claims to possess or bestow valid orders of the numerous bishops and priests classed as "*vagantes*".

specifically assigned to an urban or rural church, or to a shrine ("*martyrium*") or a monastic church. As for those who have been ordained without assignment to one of these functions [i.e., "absolutely"], the Holy Council has decided that their ordination is null and of no effect, and that, to the shame of those who conferred it, they cannot exercise their functions in any place."[24]

Of course absolute ordinations did take place before the thirteenth century, but they always met with resolute condemnation from the superior hierarchical tribunals.[25] Until the beginning of the thirteenth century it was held that any ordination *illicita* (against legal and ecclesial rules) was also *irrita* (null and void), even if the ritual of ordination was meticulously observed.

Contemporary commentators described clergy ordained in an absolute manner (for example, priests ordained for the private chapels of princes) in extremely forthright terms: they were "acephalous", "centaurs" (lay-clerics), or non-priests and non-laymen, whose very persons were living contradictions.[26]

Even in the last decade of the eleventh century, Popes and Councils alike reaffirmed the principle enunciated at Chalcedon. For instance, the Council of Piacenza (1095), under Urban II: "In accordance with sacred canons, ordination conferred absolutely is non-existent."[27]

What applies to the presbyter is equally true for the bishop consecrated outside his local church, or without any bond with the existing Church. The very meaning of the *episkopos* as head of a local church, and the essential bonds which tie him to his community, repudiate the idea of an absolute episcopal ordina-

---

[24] Ed. Lauchert, p. 90. All the Western versions (cf. Friedberg, 1, pp. 256–7), far from playing down the canon of Chalcedon, reinforce it (for example, the Dionysiana: "irritam haberi huiuscemodi manus impositionem").

[25] Leo I, *Ep. a Rusticus de Narbonne* (548), *Inq.*, 1 (*PL*, 54, 1203); Council of Pavia (850), c. 18; Urban II to the Council of Piancenza (1095), c. 15; Hugh of St Victor (v. 1140), *De sacramentis*, 11, 3, 2. Even the Romano-Germanic Pontifical of the tenth century stated that absolute ordinations were null (*PRG* 1, 10, 8, ed. Vogel-Elze).

[26] Isidore of Seville, *De eccl. officiis*, 11, 3: ". . . acephali . . . hippocentauris similes, neque equi neque homines" (*PL*, 83, 779).

[27] Council of Piacenza (1095), c. 15 (Mansi xx, 806). The term "irrita" could not, at that time, mean anything other than "null" or "non-existent".

tion.[28] It was only when the sacramental rite was viewed as mechanically conferring orders—on condition only of conformity with the liturgical books in official use (by reason of the doctrine of *opus operatum*, and quite apart from any ecclesial requirement), that absolute ordinations could be recognized. In the West, this did not occur, as I have indicated, before the Scholastic period; the Eastern churches remained faithful to the ancient tradition. Similarly, in the West before the end of the twelfth century, ordinations or other sacred actions carried out by an excommunicated, deposed, extra-diocesan, simoniac, or unworthy bishop were considered null and void. It is not difficult to see how a profound change took place in the very conception of the ministry from this date on.

IV. From Communal Penance to Private Confession

Whatever one may think of the ancient form of repentance (as practised from the third century to the end of the palaeo-Christian period), and however one may judge its rigour, uniqueness, interdictions and exclusions, one fact is beyond debate: the ancient penitential institution, a "second" baptism, was *essentially communitarian*. The three stages of the penitential process bear witness to this.[29]

Penance was commenced before the people assembled under the presidency of the bishop: the wearing of sackcloth, the imposition of the hair-shirt and ashes and the symbolic expulsion from the church were accompanied by the community's prayer. This official adoption of sinners—and not the acknowledgment of sins—was the essence of entry into the state of penitence: the sinner made neither a public nor a private *confession*.

During the penitential process, sinners had a special place in the church, were the objects of their brethren's solicitude, and formed part of an ecclesially constituted group: penitents were not withdrawn from the Christian community (sacred or civil).

[28] See the articles in the symposium *L'episcopat et l'Eglise universelle* (*Unam Sanctam* 39, Paris, 1964).

[29] In addition to the basic writings on the subject by B. Poschmann, see C. Vogel, *Esquisse sur l'évolution historique de la discipline pénitentielle dans l'Eglise Latine* (Paris and Tournai, 1961), pp. 147–235.

The only excommunication visited upon them was exclusion from eucharistic communion—but not from worship in general.[30]

When Holy Thursday, the day of reconciliation, came round, all the faithful were again present; and it was within the framework of a festal action that the bishop restored their rights to repentant sinners. Theoretically, these rights were reduced since, even though reconciled, the penitent remained under the penitential interdiction for the rest of his days. But the penitential *liturgy* and the *juridical framework* of penitence itself were quite separate.

This form of communitarian penance deserves to be called (as it so often is) "public penance", not because of the public nature of the avowal made but because of its ecclesial dimension. In fact, the main reasons for the disappearance of the ancient form of penance were the social situation of the faithful and the penitential interdictions, and not so much the inherent austerity of the penitent state. The ancient institution survived only in the form of repentance when death was imminent.[31] There should be no mistake about this: the death-bed process was the ancient form, with the three chronologically separate stages rolled into one. There was nothing like the present practice during the ancient period of Church history: all the research findings of recent years agree on this.

How then did a penitential institution, a fully communal form, come to be an individual act—the sinner's "confession" of his sins?

It happened, not by evolution, but by *substitution*. The new system—the "rating" system—was imbued with a quite different spirit.

The new discipline began to spread in Continental Europe

---

[30] The oldest sacramentaries show no sign of any of the penitential interdictions, or of any of the sequelae of penitence. See A. Chavasse, *Le sacramentaire Gelasien* (Vat. Reg., 316) (Strasbourg, 1958), pp. 140–55.

[31] This was the practice recommended, and not merely tolerated, by Caesarius of Arles and Avitus of Vienne, among others. Even a death-bed repentance involves all the juridical disqualifications associated with canonical penitence, and in the event of recovery the sinner reconciled *in extremis* has to submit to all the requirements of the canonical form. There is no connection between the repentance of the dying and private confession as now practised.

from the seventh century onwards, having been brought there from Britain, where it was elaborated without any connection with the ancient form of penitence, by the missionaries—disciples or imitators of St Columba. The essential feature of the practice was the association of each sin with a precise form of expiation (usually fasting): *so many* days, months or years of fasting for *a particular* sin. The "rates" were precisely laid down in the numerous "penitential books". As soon as the sinner had completed the fasting prescribed for his sin, he knew that the sin itself was wiped out, that an "absolution" (this term replaced "reconciliation") had (or had not) been granted him by the priest (or deacon). Clearly, *the confession* became the *essential condition* for the operation of the system: the sinner (aided or not by his "confessor"—a new term now appeared) had to give a detailed account of the sins he had committed, so that the precise penalty could be imposed on him. The essence of the system was the precisely rated form of expiation: a kind of *"do et des"* in which the legal influence is easily recognizable (the Germanic *wergeld*). Confession was still a *means*; but it was soon to become the very essence of the penitential process.

A rated form of penitence is, in theory, renewable. In fact, the fasts to be carried out, mounting up with the sins committed, often exceeded the length of a human lifetime—even for a single "confession". In addition, the rating system provided for "substitutes": masses to be said (note the connection with the rise in the number of private masses), sums of money to be paid to monasteries or churches. These "indulgences", of which many examples are recorded, provided very exactly, for example, that one year of fasting was redeemed by twenty masses, for which there was a fixed rate. The rich man could even escape the penance required for *his own* sins by having third persons fast in his place.[32] Similar examples can easily be found.

The possibility of substitute penances destroyed any effective penance on the part of the sinner, and led to scandalous abuses. Consequently, the substitutions (in fact sums of money) having eliminated all penance (even in the sordid *do et des* form), all

---

[32] See C. Vogel, "Composition légale et commutations dans le système de la pénitence tarifée", in *Revue de Droit canonique*, 8 (1958), pp. 289–318; 9 (1959), pp. 1–38, 341–359.

that remained of the tariff system was a single act on the penitent's part; that is "confession", which henceforth became the penitential process itself. Towards the end of the twelfth century, theories appeared which actually asserted that confession was the penitential act *par excellence*, by reason of the "shame and humiliation" which it brought on the sinner. From being the simple *means* it was, as an avowal, at the start of the tariff system, confession became *the* penitential process; for more than a thousand years it completely eliminated the communitarian dimension of ecclesial repentance. Given this importance of the mere avowal of sins—which, after the elimination of actual penances through the substitution system, came to stand on its own—it is easy to see how absolution could come directly after it. Expiation had lost all significance. It is also understandable that the sinner, once he had taken "confession" for penitence, and the "confessor" for the interceding community, could confess his sins (in the absence of a priest) to laymen, to objects (the knight's sword), or even to an animal (a horse). The development sketched here had run its course by the beginning of the thirteenth century; it gave rise to the system still in force in the Latin Church. It is difficult to find a sacred (or ritual) institution farther removed from its real meaning, and more alienated from the community.

For a long time, the institution was an enigma to students of its historical development: how did a message of forgiveness which was always open to the repentant sinner, but became the ancient form of penitence, then a rated form of penance, and eventually the "classic" form of "confession", manage to set restrictions on God's mercy? Tertullian was partly responsible for this disastrous degeneration.[33] It must be noted, however, that the *sacred rite*, the *liturgy* of penitence, was free of shackles which juridical prescriptions put on the mystery of reconciliation: the magnificent formularies of our sacramentaries show this clearly. In this respect, too, the alienation of the sacred action from the actuality is clear.

*   *   *

[33] Tertullian, *On Repentance*, VII, 10: "Absolution is to be given *once only* (for in fact it is already the second occasion [the first occasion having been baptism]), and never again in the future."

We can see a process of *convergence* in the development of the three forms of prayer and worship outlined above. The primitive Eucharist turned into the private mass; the presbyter's ministry culminated—by reason of a certain view of theology—in the absolute ordination; and penitence, having lost the support of the community, became individual confession. The same alienation is apparent in the three types of sacred institution.

This convergence can perhaps provide the starting-point for a resolution of the liturgical crisis—which continues despite reforms. We have to reject this division between the life of the cult and the life of the community. We must see liturgical activity as the community at prayer; and we must accept its diverse and spontaneous forms.

Translated by John Griffiths

David Power

Sacramental Celebration and Liturgical Ministry

IN this article I presuppose the theology of the assembly as treated in a previous issue of *Concilium*.[1] My concern is to provide a viewpoint from which one can consider the actual ordering of the assembly and the giving of liturgical ministry. I begin with some considerations about the individual subject. This leads us to the nature of the assembly and in turn to ministry within the assembly.

I. The Subject

In his Aquinas lecture on *The Subject* Bernard Lonergan indicated three sources from which sprang classical philosophy's neglect of the subject. These are its concern with the objectivity of truth, its notion of science as something which derives as a series of conclusions from self-evident principles, and lastly its metaphysical account of the soul.[2] In these circumstances it could show little concern with the conditions of the emergence and existence of truth, and little preoccupation with the dynamics of the advance towards truth, which are so much the theme of current philosophical endeavour.

This same contrast between the objective and the universal on the one hand and the subjective condition and development on the other marks much of our present theology's contrast with the past. This finds particular application in sacramental theology.

[1] *Concilium*, Vol. 2, n. 2 (February 1966) (American edn., Vol. 12).
[2] B. Lonergan, *The Subject* (Milwaukee, 1968), pp. 2–8.

Scholastic theology gave a metaphysical and universally applicable account of the effects of the sacraments and treated at length of their objective causality. Little was said of the subject, apart from stating the minimal requirements for the validity and fruitfulness of the sacrament. Allowance was made for the fact that the dispositions of the subject had some bearing on the effects of grace, but the implications of this were never drawn out, nor was much attention given to the conditions and process of the subject's involvement in the sacramental celebration.

More recent advances in the study of the sacraments have made it clear that much more attention is to be given to the subject. Sacramental efficacy cannot be discussed only in metaphysical and universal terms: theology has to take account of what the sacramental dialogue means in the life of the individual person, and explain how participation in celebration is conditioned by his subjective circumstances and capacities.[3]

Basic to this trend in sacramental theory is the appreciation that the human subject makes himself what he is and that he does so to the extent that his acts are the expression of the conscious self. It is through those acts which result from understanding and free choice that the person creates his own self-meaning. This is not an isolated endeavour on the part of each human person, but is determined by, and involves, the community or communities to which the individual belongs. He is called upon to give shape and meaning to his existence, to the intersubjective relations which he forges with other persons and to the world in which he lives. It is the meaning which he gives to the complexity of factors which constitute his existential situation that creates the reality of the human world in which man lives.

As revelation, the Christ-event presents the meaning of the world and of human existence as a gift from God in Christ.

[3] Cf. R. Schulte, "Sacraments", in *Sacramentum Mundi*, Vol. 5, p. 382: "... anthropology seems to offer certain bases for understanding the sacraments which is appropriate to the Christian faith. One such element ... is the very human need of 'expressing' oneself before others. ... Selfhood, one's own thoughts and volitions, seek 'expression' in and through 'another' in order to be themselves ... 'spiritual' or 'mental' attitudes, movements and reactions only become real and effective on the human, personal level when they find expression in word and gesture and create something 'other' than themselves."

Liturgy is the embodiment of this meaning in the Christian community and allows its members to take over and personally appropriate it. It does not simply confer the universal quality of grace on the subject but allows him to give new meaning to all his personal endeavour, to his interpersonal relations and to his relations with the physical universe.

This does not mean that the sacraments are concerned only with conscious understanding. They demand in the first place a belief and a trust which is an acknowledgment that the meaning of life is made possible by faith in a saving God. Because they are symbolic manifestations they allow for emotive involvement and for social identity within the body of the Church. They give an image of the world which refers all things to the pasch of Christ. They call forth creativity to the extent that as worship they reveal how human lives and institutions, and indeed the pattern of history itself, may be understood and developed in terms of the relationship between God and man which is given in Christ.

One of the difficulties about attaining an adequate and meaningful sacramental celebration is that it must not favour the impression that we are invited to escape from the everyday world into a sacred world. Liturgy should reveal to the participant the Christian meaning of his actual world. It uses traditional symbols because it must root all present meaning in the revelation of Christ, but it ought to use them in such a way as to apply them creatively to the everyday experience of the subject. If this is not done the subject can never identify with what they express, and the revelation they embody cannot become a creative force in his life.

The historical development of the liturgy reveals considerable pluriformity and independence on the part of local churches in determining their own liturgies. Recently the Second Vatican Council allowed in principle for pluriformity in sacramental celebration because of the need to give expression to the Christian message in different cultures.[4] Perhaps, however, the constitution still sees the Christian message as a relatively homogeneous set of doctrine or principles which are to be presented in

[4] Vatican II, *Sacrasanctum Concilium*, n. 37.

images and rites drawn from different cultures.[5] In fact, it is not enough to see liturgy as expressing the Christian faith in terms and images drawn from various peoples. It also has to be seen as the interpretation of the secular situation.

In this regard, our understanding of the meaning and value of human and earthly realities, our grasp of the relation of the Church to the world and of the complex problem of the connection between the Church and the kingdom of God, have vast implications for our liturgy. The Christian Gospel is not a rejection of earthly values, nor does it look askance at all human history and human progress. Its newness does not require setting up a new city or a perfect society, opposed to the city and society of man. Its newness consists rather in an interpretation which is given to the world by revealing God's love of it and by the manifestation of Christ as its alpha and omega. Liturgy must take upon itself the interpretative function of the Gospel, inasmuch as it brings home to the community and the subject the realization of Christ's presence in the world and the possibilities of dialogue with God in the city of man. Hence the reason for pluriformity in liturgy is not just that different terms and images are more comprehensible from one culture to another, but that it is grounded in the diversity of the existential situation of different communities, groups and individual persons, even within the same culture.

To see the sacraments as expressive of Christian meaning further imposes care for authenticity in their celebration as a necessary condition for their efficacy. A more traditional theology could be satisfied to state the effects of the sacraments in metaphysical terms, with universal application. Care for authenticity in celebration means that we cannot be content to determine the general significance of a sacrament, but must look for what it actually signifies in this particular case. The ritual presupposes the context within which the subject lives, and what it states about his life and the relationships which go to make it up must ring true. In other words, the various terms of the relationships

<hr>

[5] On the different viewpoints of *Sacrosanctum Concilium* and *Gaudium et Spes*, cf. J.-P. Jossua, "La Constitution 'Sacrosanctum Concilium' dans l'ensemble de l'œuvre conciliaire", in J.-P. Jossua and Y. Congar, *La Liturgie après Vatican II* (Paris, 1967), pp. 149-56.

must be verified. Vatican II and the liturgical reform have gone a long way in recognizing that rites may be adapted to the condition of the individual, e.g., in the difference between infant and adult baptism, in the anointing of the sick, and in penance. The liturgy does not present persons with abstract possibilities of grace, but with an interpretation of their world in which the possibilities of grace are revealed, and so may be grasped and accepted in response to this revelation.

II. COMMUNITY

It is of the very core of sacramental meaning that Christians are united together as communion through their belief in Christ, and that the individual subject is united with God in and through the community. If, in fact, there is no such reality and no experience of this communion in the life of the subject, for him its symbolic expression in the liturgy remains void, and does not in any way present him with the possibility of pursuing the potentialities of such community in his daily life.

It is sometimes asked whether liturgy presupposes or creates community, but the answer is that liturgy can only create community if it already exists in some measure. It is the sense of oneness which brings Christians together in worship in the first place: to express, explore and increase their communion. Even baptism cannot be entered into except by someone who has already forged links with the community and who is ready at this stage to commit himself totally in faith to it, and to the dialogue with God which its membership permits.

Acts 2. 42–46 enables us to understand in some measure what the liturgical assembly presupposes in terms of the experience of community.[6] The common life of the Jerusalem community entailed not only praying and breaking bread together but some communal possession of goods, at least to the extent that nobody was suffered to go in want. This practical aspect of fellowship is a necessary constituent of community, and a necessary presupposition for the liturgical assembly if it is to be an authentic celebration of Christian communion. The table-fellowship of the

[6] Cf. S. Lyonnet, "La Nature du Culte dans le Nouveau Testament", *ibid.*, pp. 357–67.

disciples with Christ during his earthly life, which reached a culminating point in the Last Supper of the twelve with him, represents the ideal of all community in Christ.

This sense of fellowship evidently entails mutual concern and
mutual service, a point which is brought out in the image of the
Church as Christ's body. There is no real sense of community unless it is expressed in a mutual service modelled on the Son of
Man who gave his life for the many. If this prerequisite for
liturgy is lacking, what is said in the sacraments about relations
to Christ, to the Father, to the Spirit, to one another or to the
world, is simply not true. The symbols may be very exactly
posited, and the liturgical actions well performed, but if they do
not ring true in the context of the life of those celebrating, because of the absence of the experience of Christian community
in the celebrants' lives, the meaning of life expressed in them
cannot be appropriated. In other words, in such circumstances
the subject is not able, and his own subjective make-up is not
such, that he can grasp whatever reality is expressed in the sacramental celebration, and so there is no possibility of his expressing
himself in those terms.

At the same time, because the advance to truth and growth in
charity is an ongoing process, the community's (and the individual's within the community) self-expression in the liturgy
is also a self-creation. It is by coming to a greater consciousness
of the self and the self's potentialities that man makes himself,
provided this consciousness is not mere abstract intellectualism
but is evaluative and expressive of willing endeavour. It is by
serving as expression of Christian self-identity and by opening up
a creative interpretation of Christian fellowship that liturgy enables a community, and the individual in the community, to advance in faith and love in such a way that this opens up new
possibilities for the life of the Christian fellowship in the world.

III. ORDER IN THE ASSEMBLY

It is because the assembly must be a growth in Christian awareness that this assembly has to reflect and represent a whole church
order. This is the implication of the traditional belief that the
Church is most truly itself in the moment of liturgical assembly,

a tradition dating from the New Testament that was so strong that it identified Church and assembly, and found the actuality of the Church of God in the eucharistic gathering of the local community of disciples.

The order within the assembly expresses the view which the community has of relationships within it and of its relationship to Christ. If we reflect upon the historical development of the episcopacy, we can see that the importance of the episcopacy in the whole life of the community with regard to discipline and doctrine is correlative with his importance in the Eucharist. His presidency of the one goes with his presidency of the other, and the saying that the bishop is in the Church and the Church in the bishop applies equally to one case and to the other.[7] The strict hierarchical structure of the liturgical assembly put forward by Ignatius, Cyprian or Hippolytus reflects their ideas of order within the community. No doubt it both sprang from and gave fresh vigour to this order.

Studies of church order in the New Testament and in the early Church warn us to be careful about describing the origins of liturgical ministry and about the relations which we posit between liturgical and extra-liturgical offices. But in the emergence of the episcopacy as this took place in the second and third Christian centuries there is a clear relation between the two. The bishop is head of the church and high-priest of the assembly; he is sign and source of unity in both respects. A more freely structured assembly would be evidence of a more freely structured church. Structure and freedom are two different factors to keep in balance, but it is on the maintenance of this balance that a flourishing church life depends.

Liturgical development has tended in the Roman Catholic Church in the direction of strict order, and the role of the ordained minister has in many respects eclipsed any other ministry. The Second Vatican Council has called for greater, more conscious and more active participation from the faithful, and this call is in keeping with the idea of a church community in which laity as well as clergy have an active part. Despite the recent changes, however, in liturgical rites the church assembly remains

[7] Cyprian, Ep. 66, 8.

a very structured one, and one in which the role of the ordained
minister is on the one hand predominant but on the other hand
bound fast by official rulings.

At the present juncture, a double alienation between assembly
and community experience seems possible. On the one hand, if
the laity are invited to contribute to a more active worship, in
which they may act as readers, organist, choir-master, and so on,
they will find it strange if they are expected to keep silent on
other matters of church life. In other words, even the rather
meagre amount of lay activity which is already possible in liturgy
requires a church order which allows for lay participation in
other matters of common welfare, and the sense of community
which is expected in the liturgy calls for that measure of common
life which makes it ring true. But on the other hand, where a
group of Christians are trying to live a life of more intense fellowship, and where a more free and democratic relationship between
laity and clergy has been achieved, the official liturgical structures readily seem inadequate as a mode of self-expression and
creation. This is the basic reason behind unofficial assemblies and
unauthorized liturgical experimentation. It is the quest for the
suitable symbolic manifestation of an ideal of Christian fellowship. A church order which allows dialogue and creative initiative on the part of all necessitates a liturgy which allows the
same, since this is the moment in which the community under-
stands, realizes and creates itself.

We must resist the temptation to idealize early church order
(perhaps not always accurately interpreted at that), but there are
some factors in the worship of the early Church which may help
us to understand how it could create a fellowship of mutual and
active concern. In speaking of the assembly of the Corinthian
church, Paul was no doubt struck by its abuses and wished to
correct a number of these. Yet the correlation between the multiplicity of ministries in the community and a similar multiplicity
in the assembly is striking. In the one case and in the other, there
is the decided impression that contributions to the common life
(of mutual concern or of worship) were forthcoming from many
directions, and that this was taken as evidence of the freedom of
the Spirit working in the Church. Something of the same free
and diversified contribution to worship needs to be introduced

into our assemblies today, though perhaps in different form. It is needful to remember that the approach taken to matters like the dialogue homily, singing, church music, free prayer or dance, concerns not only an isolated world of cult but the image of the church fellowship which is mirrored in this worship and which it serves to create. The faithful cannot be simply asked to perform such services according to given instructions and official texts, but much has to be left to their own creativity.

To grasp the dialogal and creative nature of the assembly at worship, it is necessary to appreciate the primacy of the word in the life of the Church and the presence of the Spirit for the hearing of the word. The Church is before all else the community of believers, who have heard and responded to the Word of God made known to us in Jesus Christ. Religious ritual is the memorial and celebration of the "word believed" by the Christian community. It is first and foremost in the assembly that it must become clear that the word is given to all of Christ's members, and that the creative understanding, assimilation and proclamation of this word which is the work of the Spirit are in some measure and in different ways shared by each and all. In the ritual, the whole community exercises the service of the word, and the meaningful entry of God's word into the life of the community and of its individual members. This means that anybody has a liturgical ministry to perform, who either by word of proclamation or by word of explanation or by word of prayer (in word, song or dance) is able to express something of the meaning of life for those present as it is interpreted and received in the light of the original Christ-event.

IV. The Ordained Ministry

The role of the special ministry conferred by ordination can be seen within the context of the assembly as symbolic of the diaconal and dialogal nature of the church community. Whatever liturgical ministry is exercised by ordained persons in the assembly is symbolic of some broader ministry to be exercised in the life of the church community. It has already been remarked that the early origins of eucharistic and liturgical ministry are obscure, as is the connection between church order and the order of the assembly. But there is obviously some parallel between one and the other, and the combination of the presidency of the church and the Eucharist in the person of the bishop seems a logical and natural evolution, even though it may in time have unfortunately tended to suppress the total or free expression of other members of the community.

Just as we have mentioned the primacy of the word in the life of the Church, so recent studies on the ministry give great importance to the ordained minister's service of the word, and this line of approach was taken up by the Fathers of the Second Vatican Council. This is excellent, inasmuch as it recognizes the importance of the word in the life of the Church and even links the gospel of the word with its ritual celebration. But if ordination is then seen as necessary for a mission to preach the word, there is an unwarranted restriction of this service to a category of persons in the Church. In so far as it is possible to draw definite conclusions from the New Testament, it would seem that the apostolic, prophetic and didactic ministries of the word were not necessarily connected with a delegation by the laying-on of hands, and hence these word-ministries were not the prerogative of ordained persons.

It might be more correct to suggest that the link between ordination and the ministry of word and Eucharist is the result of a necessary institutionalization of ministry and office. Proclamation of word and ritual act are both of themselves in the nature of passing events. They have to be constantly repeated and renewed, and this must be done in sundry places and at sundry times. Some tangible bond or link between the many events of proclamation and celebration is needed so that the community may have a sense of coherence, continuity and unity, and so that it may attain its own self-identity in fidelity to the one word which is thus so variously presented and commemorated. Institutionalization is necessary in any society if it is to retain its self-identity and its capacity to be self-perpetuating. This is also why church institutions are necessary, including that of the ordained ministry of word and sacrament. What has sometimes unfortunately occurred is that the presence of Christ and the power of God's word have been almost identified with the institutionalized ministry. It has at times been seen only as a spiritual power, and practically as the sole possessor of a spiritual power, instead of being appreciated in its nature as sign and role. As sign and role its purpose is to serve the presence of Christ and his word in the community, wherever this presence may manifest itself. It is a bond in both space and time which gives unity to all the different manifestations of the word, so that each is linked with the apostolic succession of the church community and with the catholicity of the churches.

In every society there are some roles in which function and representation go hand in hand. Because the function concerns some very important aspect of life in the society, the person who exercises it becomes a representative of this aspect of the society. An example of this is the role and function of a judge in a court of law; because he presides over legal actions he, along with his fellow members of the judiciary, symbolizes the legal bonds which serve the common good. Indeed, there are some roles whose purpose is primarily symbolic, not functionary, and to which it belongs to represent the total community and institution. Such is the role of a king in a constitutional monarchy or that of the president of a republican state. The functions of such a person represent the self-understanding of a community or society. In every case of a representative role, its existence makes it possible for the citizens to identify with the society or the aspect of the society thus represented and it provides the society with a sense of stability and continuity. These roles are of particular importance in times of crisis, for they can either help or hinder a transition in the self-understanding and development of a community, by reason of the role-personage's readiness to change his attitude to his function in order to represent the new development or else of his resistance to change.

Some understanding of the need for ordained ministers in the ministry of word and liturgy can be obtained on the basis of this comparison. According to the Second Vatican Council, the ordained priest is the sacramental expression of Christ's headship over his Church.[8] This representative role is made apparent in the exercise of the ministry, and in this ministry the priest represents the total Christian community in its submission to the headship

---

[8] Vatican II, *Presbyterorum Ordinis*, n. 2.

of Christ. The ordained minister represents Christ as head inasmuch as he represents the Church's acknowledgment of this headship, in a way analogous to that in which Christ represents God the Father by representing man's acknowledgment of and accession to the Father. It is a common tenet of theology that Christ represents God to man and man to God. Recent thought on the question speaks of Christ revealing God to man by revealing man to himself, in terms of his dynamic striving to give himself and to come to God. It was by dying and rising as man in obedience to the Father and in testimony to love's rejection of sin that he revealed the Father to men, for in that action he showed the Father to be lord of life and death, lord of human existence because lord of Jesus Christ and the Saviour who has the power to conquer the evil of sin and death. Analogously, the ordained minister represents Christ to the community inasmuch as he represents the community's obedience to Christ as God's Word. By revealing the community to itself as dependent on Christ, he reveals Christ. Hence his role in the community is to represent the self-identity of the community as a gathering of those who believe in Jesus Christ and accept him as God's Word, and in this way acknowledge his headship. The special ministry of ordination is to serve this self-understanding of the Christian community: not just by offices and functions, but as symbol.

Whether it concerns the ministry of the word, the assembly for worship, or the discipline of community life, one of the earliest notions associated with the special ministry conferred by the laying-on of hands is that of presidency. To say that someone presides over an activity is very different to saying that he is the unique source of that activity. In the Church, the inspiration for the life of the community could come from all those who possessed the charism of the word, whether apostles, prophets or learned men. The care of community needs was readily satisfied by the grace and charity of many members. Since Christianity continues the religious tradition of Judaism, wherein family ritual was so common, and since it gave an emphasis to domestic liturgy in preference to temple service, it may not in the beginning have seemed necessary to reserve all ritual celebrations to appointed leaders or ministers. But some coherence, some indication and effector of unity and order, is necessary in any society or community, and it is likely that presidential bodies or repre-sentative persons were appointed within the local communities in response to such needs.

In this sense, it would seem correct to say that the history of the Church's hierarchical ministry is the history of the institu-tionalization of the *diakonia* and the setting-up of roles necessary for the continuity of faith and the self-identity of believing Chris-tians as a community which is both local and universal. Despite a continuity in names from the second century to the present day, it cannot be asserted that the roles to which the names are attached have remained unchanged, or that there is one particu-lar form of institutionalized ministry which is divinely deter-mined and immutable.[9] What Christ gave to his Church was his word and his Spirit. That there should be a ritual commemora-tion of this word, to keep it alive and transmit it through that apt symbolism which is necessary for the transmission of any re-ligious belief, and that there should be institutionalized roles of leadership and ministry in the community of his followers, fol-lows from the very nature of the Church as community. Both the ritual and the institutions are bound to have their roots in Christ's deeds and words, as well as in the community life of his early followers, but, as long as this necessary grounding in the Christ-event is maintained, both the ritual and the institutions are subject to considerable variation.

In its document on the liturgy, Vatican II gives the principle that the most exemplary form of liturgical gathering is that held under the presidency of the diocesan bishop, and the presidency of the priest in the parish or other community is referred to the bishop.[10] In theory, we can see the point of this approach. If in fact the bishop is the centre of community in his diocese and this belongs to the experience of community which the faithful bring with them to the assembly, then he therein represents their mutual cohesion and their cohesion with other churches. In

---

[9] There seems to be a growing consensus about the legitimacy of dif-ferent ministerial structures. Cf. *Lutherans and Catholics in Dialogue*: Vol. 4, *Eucharist and Ministry* (Washington and New York, 1970), p. 15: "We are agreed that the basic reality of the apostolic Ministry can be preserved amid variations in structure and implementation, in rites of ordination and in theological explanation."

[10] Vatican II, *Sacrosanctum Concilium*, nn. 41, 42.

practice, however, it must be admitted that the sense of community in a diocese is often inexistent, or at least does not play a large part in the lives of the faithful. Therefore the local gathering is of greater factual importance in giving the sense of community since it provides a more tangible reality to the participants and a greater opportunity for the subject to come to Christian maturity and self-expression. This points to the importance of the presidency of such gatherings and of the communities which are therein assembled.

It is important to appreciate in history and in present developments the influence which the community has on the changing nature of the ordained ministry. As in every human society, there is at least a measure in which the church community creates its own roles, determines their functions and changes them with the march of time. As beliefs and traditions develop, and with these the community's self-understanding, there is also a change in the role which the ordained minister must play.

The community cannot, of course, change the nature and function of the ministry at will, or by simple caprice. Once the role has been created, the community in a sense has handed itself over to the leadership of the one filling it, and his charge is peculiarly one of unity and continuity—which, let it be said, is not always best exercised by way of preserving tradition but is often more necessarily a guidance to development in continuity with the past and in communion with other churches. It is the believing community, past, present and future, which is represented by the ordained ministry, and the authority they possess from Christ is to exercise this role in appropriate fashion, by the signs, words and actions which best serve the living presence of the Word in the community of the present, which is necessarily linked up with both past and future. But since the Christian community itself must develop if it is to serve the presence of God in the world, the role of the ordained ministry must also develop, and this development cannot be the exclusive concern or doing of the hierarchy. It is the operation of the entire community, since the meaning given to the ministry changes with the meaning and self-understanding of the community itself. This is so because the role assigned to the minister is one of the chief expressions of the community's self-understanding. The meaning of the ministry and its corresponding functions are determined in terms of how it may best serve the presence and mission of the Church as a sign of God's presence in the world. Whatever change is postulated in the ministry in times of crisis may involve self-emptying and catharsis and conversion on the part of the ministers, but it is a necessity for the developing life of the Church.

We are clearly living through such a period of crisis at present, when not only the Church but the whole world, the culture and modes of thought and living of our times, are changing. There is much personal confusion and disaffection when those in public roles seem to represent by their activity a different kind of belief and community to what many hope for and expect. The ordained ministers of the Church can help the transition by the way in which they exercise their office, including their liturgy, and now-adays particularly by being more alive to word than law, to challenge than immutable tradition, to co-operation and creativity than to discipline, and to the world than to flight from it. Within the assembly this means an attentiveness to the contribution of all present, in ways that have been indicated already in this article.

V. The Presence of Christ

I have said above that the liturgy expresses and creates the Christian community because it is an interpretation of the meaning of Christian presence in the world, and so provides the subject with the means whereby to come to an effective and creative awareness of his Christian faith. Christ is present in the sacramental signs and symbols. It is not just a question of the signs making known what is otherwise true and present, but the signs themselves constitute the mode of communication and presence. But the symbolic presence of Christ in the liturgy is not concerned only with the intercommunication between him and the faithful which is achieved through this presence. It is also a revelation and an interpretation of his presence in the continuing fellowship of his Church as sacrament of his presence in the world.

The Vatican Council mentions the many signs of Christ's

presence in the liturgy, and we know that the particular efficacy of a liturgical action comes from the extent to which it sacramentally manifests the Christian mystery.[11] It is through these signs that we come to grasp and understand the reality of Christ's presence in the Church and in the world. The eucharistic presence of Christ is the most revelatory, because it is brought about through the greatest and most telling complexity of signs and symbols. Because the ritual makes use of the human realities of fellowship in a meal, and of the bread and wine, symbols of man's life and toil, it reveals to us the presence of Christ in all created reality and the fact that he gives himself to the world, transforming it by his love. Since his presence in the symbols of bread and wine is related to his presence in the assembly gathered in faith, this is a sign that his presence in the world is discovered in the dialogue situation of the believing community, joined together in faith and mutual service. Since the Eucharist is presided over by an ordained minister, this gathering also shows that Christ reveals his presence in the world in a Church which is organically disposed, and maintains apostolic succession, unity and universality through the mediation of the institutional factor of an ordained ministry. In brief, the fullest and the most interpretative sign of the meaning of the universe in terms of Christ's pasch is in the transformation of the bread and wine into the body and blood of Christ by the prayer of an assembly gathered together under the presidency of an ordained minister, acting as its head and representative within the unity of the universal Church. This is the supreme moment of presence because it is the supreme moment of communion with the meaning of life which is embodied in the pasch and the supreme moment of discovery of those conditions under which Christ is encountered in life.

It is clear that Christ is not present only in an assembly in which an ordained minister presides. It is also clear that his presence is not brought about only by the action of the ordained minister. What has been attempted in this article is to indicate what is signified by the presence and action of an ordained minister in the assembly, and then to see how this affects the nature

[11] *Ibid.*, n. 7.

of communication with Christ in the sacramental symbols, since the ministry itself belongs to the order of sacrament and symbol.

In pastoral practice we must always remain aware of the subject and of the conditions and circumstances which will allow the particular community or individual person to come to an awareness of the Christian faith and its demands, and thus to enter into communion with Christ. This may not always be in fact in the perfectly structured liturgical assembly. Wherever any of the signs of Christ's presence are to be found, he is himself present, but the recognition of these signs by the subject does depend in large measure on his experience and background and it must be asked what they signify here and now for this subject or this gathering, since only their conscious recognition makes communion with Christ possible. Consequently many types of Christian gathering for worship, more or less structured, remain a practical necessity.[12] Desire for the ideal should not lead to the suppression of the real.

[12] Cf. D. Power, "Home or Group Prayer and the Divine Office", *Concilium*, Vol. 2, no. 6 (February 1970), pp. 94–7 (American edn., Vol. 52).

Pedro Tena

The Liturgical Assembly
and its President

ST BENEDICT, writing about the role of the abbot, coined a happy
phrase that has become classic: *"oportet prodesse magis quam
praeesse"*. He who presides does so for the benefit of the assembly,
"exercising authority with anxious care" (Rom. 12. 8). It is not
by accident that the term "president" to denote the presbyter or
bishop at the eucharistic celebration has become prevalent at the
present time; it is because we have once again come to see that
liturgical action is not a private function—whether the "private
person" is a presbyter or a bishop—but a "celebration of the
Church, which is...a holy people united and organized under
its bishops" (*Const. on the Liturgy*, 26).

The more one stresses the Church as the subject of the liturgy,
the clearer it becomes that the president's role in a liturgical
assembly is conditioned by what the Church wants that celebration to do. Hence it is not possible to talk about the president of
the assembly without first considering the assembly as such, start-
ing from its character as "church of God" (cf. 1 Cor. 2. 17–22).
Only after that can one form a more accurate view of the characteristics of the person who has the mission of presiding at it,
and the way in which he should behave.

I. THE LITURGICAL ASSEMBLY

This is not the place for a general consideration of the assembly
as such, which has already been examined elsewhere.[1] Here, I

[1] See *Concilium*, February 1966.

43

want to study it only from one aspect, which can be summed up in the question: what are the necessary elements for the correct functioning of the liturgical assembly?

I should make clear at the outset that I am considering liturgical assemblies in general, and not just the eucharistic assembly, although it is here that the content of the Christian assembly is most clearly manifested. For the same reason, I do not propose to touch on the relationship between the common priesthood of the faithful and the ministerial priesthood. This means taking a broad view which will have to be detailed at some points, but should be borne in mind throughout the following considerations. Every liturgical assembly has to be seen in three dimensions at the same time: (1) As the action of a Christian community, and so from the viewpoint of faith; (2) as the action of a group of persons whose particular characteristic is that they form a religious group, and so have characteristics that can be studied by psychology and sociology; (3) as an action taking place in history, and consequently with emphases peculiar to *this* Christian community, or *that* group of persons, in their own particular setting, relating to a certain set of events, certain cultural influences, and so on.

1. *Functional Elements of the Christian Community*

The centre of every liturgical assembly is clearly the Lord (Mt. 18. 20), and so the element on which all the others must depend is clearly the confessed faith of the assembled community. A community of "saints" should be made up of those who believe in their hearts and profess in their words that God raised the Lord Jesus from the dead (Rom. 10. 9). One cannot conceive of a liturgical assembly made up of "anonymous" or "implicit" Christians; these, by definition, cannot make up a Christian assembly, which is essentially a public and explicit act. We all know of the difficulties posed by liturgical assemblies made up of Christians whose belief in the heart is weak and whose profession in words seems to have no effect on the rest of their lives. This is one of the most acute of all pastoral problems, but one that we cannot go into here. Suffice to stress that a liturgical assembly stems from faith, or rather, is itself a confession of faith in the Lord.

The visible representation of this central element is usually through the proclamation of the word of God, with all this signifies and involves: a proclamation that recalls all those "called to be saints" (1 Cor. 1. 2), to place them once more in their original position as hearers of the word, not leaving them as an ordinary human group. This is followed by the setting of the community in the here and now through the homily; the reception of the word, expressed in various ways, and so on.

The constant, definitive, subject of the Word of God is the *agape* of God revealed in the paschal mystery of Jesus Christ, prefigured in the Scriptures, and its message is an exhortation to us to live this *agape*. In this way the word shows a third functional element in every liturgical assembly: love of the brethren, as Christ loved us (Jn. 13. 34–5). A liturgical assembly cannot "consist" without love as a radical element permeating the whole of it. I stress the point in order to affirm this Christian love and at the same time to distinguish it from the efforts at mutual acceptance that any group must make if it is to remain united. The themes of ecclesial ministry as an act of love (cf. Jn. 21. 17) and of the president as servant (cf. Lk. 22. 24–7, Jn. 13. 13–16) relate directly to this element of the assembly, as do the presence and influence of the Holy Spirit, since it is the Holy Spirit who pours God's love into our hearts (Rom. 5. 5).

From this basis of the trilogy Lord-faith, word-response and Spirit-*agape*, we can now pass on to two new functional elements of the assembly.

Through being an ecclesial community, the liturgical assembly is linked and open to other assemblies, and, through its members, linked and open also to all men; it is catholic. If it were not, it would become a sect. As it exists in time and space, each liturgical assembly should feel willing to accept new contributions, and should be deeply conscious of being the recipient of a tradition that outlasts it. A liturgical assembly never starts from zero, nor does it have to reinvent its *raison d'être*. While it affirms its particular being-in-history, without which it would lose its identity, it does so in communion, linking with previous generations and opening out to future ones; it accepts contemporary pluralism precisely because it knows that underlying it is a deep and unbreakable unity.

At the same time, the liturgical assembly knows itself to be an "institution", that is, a public fact in the Church. When the Christian community meets together as such, it does not stop being a sign of the Church at the same time. "Liturgical services pertain to the whole body of the Church; they manifest it and have effects upon it..." (*Const. on the Liturgy*, 26). So, whatever form it may take, the liturgical assembly always remains the responsibility of the pastors of the Church, those whose task is to ensure the continuance of the faith of the apostle (*Const. on the Church*, 26). This is not a matter of exercising a juridical or bureaucratic authority, but the Church must always be able to say whether a particular liturgical assembly is truly apostolic. This element, like the previous one, is a condition for the functioning of the assembly; their importance should not be underestimated.

There is one last functional element: joy. The absence-presence of the Lord in the midst of his people has always produced this feeling in the hearts of Christians, right from the beginning. From the community in Jerusalem, who "Day by day ... breaking bread in their homes, partook of food with glad and generous hearts" (Acts 2. 46), to the festive chants of the most way-out folk mass, joy—the feast—has always been the way faith and love expressed themselves. Of course, when we say "joy"— just as when we say "love"—we are not talking of the purely psychological aspects, but of eschatological ones; but this does not mean that the latter should not promote the former: quite the reverse.

2. *Functional Elements of the Assembly as Religious Community*

The liturgical assembly is first a human group, and then, more specifically, a group whose objective is a religious activity. When the elements that determine the correct functioning of such groups are applied to the liturgical assembly, this should be done with the particular nature of the community of faith always in mind, as well as the transitory nature of an assembly, particularly if its numbers are large.[2]

The feeling of belonging possessed by members of the group

[2] Cf. R. Echarren, "La presidencia cultual entre el sectarismo y la comunidad cristiana", in *Presidir la asamblea* (Madrid, 1970), pp. 159–93. Cf. also "Liturgie et sciences humaines", in *La Maison-Dieu* 91 (1967), pp. 65–162.

is a first and basic element; unless this is present it is not properly speaking possible to talk of a group at all. A true community of action will only be found when the group is able to speak of itself in the plural, as "us". The best way of reaching this desirable goal is to clarify the objectives that the group sets itself. The aim binds the members of the group together and gives them experience of the feeling of belonging. With a transitory meeting, it is even more important to establish the "wherefore" of its coming together, as there is no previous link between its members.

But a definition of objectives does not exhaust the matter. There are still two elements necessary for correct integration in a group: feeling oneself recognized and accepted as a member of the group, and genuine personal participation in the tasks the group undertakes to achieve its particular aim. These two elements are not to be seized unilaterally, but depend for their achievement on a joint effort on behalf of the community and each new member who wishes to become integrated into it. There is a whole gamut of interpersonal relationships that has to come into play. A personal attitude of openness to others is absolutely necessary if one is to feel accepted as a member. This aspect is particularly interesting in the liturgical assembly, even if it is fulfilled there, not only on the psychological level, but on the level of the spirit of faith. The assembly cannot function properly with some of its members locked in individualism: in the long run, in fact, one would be forced to conclude that those who remain closed up cannot even call themselves Christians, since they lack the necessary minimum of openness to the Word of God calling and inviting them from outside, and summoning them to conversion and an open heart.

On the other hand, it is not the same thing as a group of friends, or a work group, or a common-interest group. For, to participate in it, each member requires a clear appreciation of the situation of the group itself, and a sincere disposition—clearly recognized too—to put at the service of the community what he knows he can bring to it.

Acceptance or otherwise of the symbolism of the group is another particular element that affects its integration. "Studies of the sociology of ritual clearly demonstrate the integrating role of acts of worship. Ritual should be seen as a form of symbolical communication.... Ritual has a power of binding together; it is opposed to anonymity, creates a feeling of 'us', because it identifies. Besides its theological purposes, ritual has a latent sociological purpose: integration into a social structure, and also differentiation of status and function in the bosom of the community of the faithful."[3] In the case of the liturgical assembly, this element has particular consequences at times like the present, when symbolism is tending to diversify along regional lines, in order to adapt itself better to the character of the local assembly. Such an adaptation has consequences that should be seriously thought about.

3. *Functional Elements of the Community as an Historical Community*

Just as the Church only exists in history through the medium of Christian communities, so the liturgical assembly only exists through every legitimate meeting of Christians coming together in the name of the Lord. This is why, when examining the functional elements of the assembly, one has to come back to an examination of a particular assembly. Not, of course, to judge the validity of elements valid for a religious community, or a religious group, by their application to a particular assembly—a sort of "situation theology"—but to actualize them in a definite dimension. This is where theology begins its dialogue with psychology and sociology, with culture and politics.[4]

It would be impossible to undertake an examination of liturgical assemblies in their historical manifestation here. I can only hope to indicate a few points of reference that are most widely applicable in the present situation.

First, liturgical assemblies are oscillating between homogeneity and heterogeneity. The principle behind this diversity can be seen from many different angles: in ages, in culture, in religious, political or social ideology.... Which means, in short, that pluralism has to be taken into account. The consequence is that the greater the heterogeneity, the deeper the integrating elements

---

[3] Echarren, *op. cit.*, pp. 162-3.
[4] See Y. Congar, "Authorité, initiative, coresponsabilité", in *La Maison-Dieu* 97 (1969), pp. 34-57.

have to be. At almost every moment, the aims of the meeting on one hand, and the affirmation of faith and love on the other, have to be deliberately brought out.

Secondly, liturgical assemblies vary in size. This is an important factor, of concern principally to psychologists, since it conditions the manner in which members of the group behave, their participation and integration. It also, of course, conditions the way the meeting itself is organized and the part played by its president, with all the consequences this involves.[5]

Thirdly, liturgical assemblies can vary very considerably according to the purposes they are designed to serve. An assembly held in the parish church to celebrate the Sunday mass is not the same thing as a monastic community meeting for vespers. The attitudes of the members of each group will be very different, and each requires a different treatment. The one may easily contain people who go to seek, preferably with a certain degree of anonymity, an individual moment of security and religious fervour, while the other will normally be made up of people willing to participate, to integrate themselves into the group, and to express their faith in common.

Apart from these pluralisms, our age imposes certain anthropological constants, experience of which will of course vary in intensity between different assemblies, but which are none the less real and even universal to a certain degree. One of these, for example, is the sense of democracy. The mystery of the authority that structures a group is less and less apparent to men today, and there is no reason to deny that this fact represents a positive value, provided it encourages the members of a community to feel responsible for their own part, played according to their particular qualifications.

A critical attitude to authoritarianism is another constant: one might call it a sort of "diffused Oedipus complex", leading to the "death of the father" being sought as the natural solution to any attempt to impose institutional authority. The feeling for the freedom and integrity of the individual is a third constant, and

---

[5] One could, at this point, go into the whole question of celebrations in small groups, and the psychological requirements in such cases. On the liturgical aspect of this, see *Phase* 52, devoted to "Liturgy and basic communities", and *Comunidades de base y expresión de la fe* (Barcelona, 1970).

this plays a very important part at the moment of bringing people together into a group, since it makes it more difficult to establish activity in common, although once this has been achieved it should be more intense through being freely accepted by all those taking part.

Finally, a fourth constant could be the feeling for efficiency that dominates most people's thought today as a result of technological progress. This is obviously very influential in the basic decision to accept any form of liturgical activity at all—since it serves no utilitarian purpose, it is no "use" to anyone. This can lead either to a radical challenge to the whole idea of the assembly, or to an attempt to "make use" of the assembly in pursuit of aims that do not properly belong to it.

Besides these anthropological constants, it should be recognized that there are also ecclesial features peculiar to our age: a pluralism of communities, a greater variety of choice being exercised by Christians, an atmosphere of change, opposed factions within religions, etc. This situation is undoubtedly bound to have its effect on our liturgical assemblies.

*   *   *

All these groups of elements lead us to an answer to our initial question: what is needed for the correct functioning of a liturgical assembly? Based on the answers given, we must now pass on to the president of the assembly, and ask what characteristics he should have in order to set all these elements in motion or at least help them to function, who he should be, and how he should act to carry out his function correctly.

II. The President of the Assembly

The word "president" (*proistámenos*) in the New Testament is used with reference to the ministerial function (cf. Rom. 12. 8; 1 Thess. 5. 12; 1 Tim. 5. 17, 3. 12, 3. 4–5; Tit. 3. 8, 14). In all these texts, its meaning is "being responsible for", "guiding", "having care of".... It is a humble word, technically imprecise, and capable of expressing the novelty of the Christian celebration and the meaning of the assembly; it is a functional word, denoting a function in relation to a group.

1. *Rules for choosing the President of a Liturgical Assembly*

The rules under discussion are of course theological, and the first is the rule of what I would call the "sacramentality" of the assembly. The Church is made visible in every assembly, although to differing degrees. The characteristics of the person responsible (= the president) depend on the ecclesial level on which the assembly takes place. The *who* is conditioned by the *what*. The greater the ecclesial entity of a communitary action, the greater the total presence of the pastoral responsibility of the Church. It is just this sacramental dimension that must determine which member of the assembly should exercise the presidency, not any other qualities he might possess (including his possession or otherwise of personal holiness). This has the danger that it can lead to dissociation of ministry from holiness, and sometimes to a certain distance between the president and the assembly; but one has to bear in mind that the assembly is a public act of the Church, that ministry also carries a charism, and that the basis of each assembly is "one Lord" (Eph. 4. 5).[6]

The second rule is that of ecclesial communion: a liturgical assembly needs to be open to all the dimensions of charity, and cannot allow anyone to be responsible for it if he lacks this openness. This is a rule full of practical applications in our day, because while one cannot admit the authenticity of liturgical assemblies that exclude ecclesial communion, one has to draw a line between the pluralism of communities and the limits of ecclesial communion.

A third rule would be the rule of gratuitousness. The more closely a liturgical assembly aligns its objective with its possibilities as a Christian community, the more democratic it can be in its choice of president. So, if it has no aim other than to express what it is, its president can be selected from among those present. But when it hopes to receive the gratuitous saving grace of God in Christ (as in the Eucharist), then its president should be someone who, within the community, personally represents sacramental-hierarchical mediation: that is, he must be a Christian sufficiently "characterized" in the Church through "ordination" to act *in persona Christi capitis*. This rule carries the danger of being

---

[6] Cf. P. Tena, "El planteamiento de la función presidencial en la actualidad", in *Presidir la asamblea, op. cit.*, pp. 17-43.

interpreted aristocratically as a concession to the "powers", or as a "magical" sense of hierarchical intervention, so it is absolutely essential that it should always be seen in the context of Christian worship as a profession of faith in the Church.

This leads to another rule: the rule of guarantee of the faith of the Church. Presiding at family prayer and presiding at the Eucharist are two very different things, but both impose the responsibility for seeing that that particular communitary action fulfils its aim: to be an act of worship in the faith of the Church. The person who presides at a liturgical assembly is the guarantor and promoter of the ecclesial identity of the activity, which is to say that on the liturgical level he carries out the function that belongs to the hierarchy over the whole of church life. A gathering for family prayer would not involve the faith of the Church so decisively as a eucharistic celebration, though it is of course a good thing that Christians should follow the model of the pastoral magisterium in their own prayers.

2. *Rules for the President's Behaviour*

Knowing who should preside at the assembly is only one step towards its proper functioning: one also has to know how this president should behave to give coherence to the whole.[7]

As a first general observation: he cannot be responsible for the assembly unless he thinks of the Church as a communion and the presidency as a service. No one in the whole world is master of the faith of the brethren (cf. 2 Cor. 1. 24). The practical applications of this basic rule are innumerable. One example would be the president's faithfulness to the purpose of a particular assembly; each assembly, from a prayer meeting to the Eucharist, has its own direction, and the president must clarify this direction in such a way as to allow the integration of its members, being careful that the objective is not obscured, nor the approach of the community distorted. Above all, he must keep a close watch on

[7] The approach taken in this article does not claim to deal directly with the functioning of an assembly from the standpoint of group dynamics (leadership, etc.), so as not to limit the application of these rules of behaviour, which I have tried to place in as broad a context as possible, so that they are, I believe, valid for any assembly, large or small. For a directly psychological approach, see A. Jiménez, "Las técnicas de la dinámica de grupo al servicio de la asamblea liturgica", in *Presidir la asamblea*, pp. 197–204.

himself, to ensure that he does not impose his own purpose on the community, which would spoil the communitary purpose.

Coming down to more practical details, the president cannot allow himself to "personalize" the assembly at which he presides, except from motives of real fidelity to the assembly; so the choice of texts, fidelity to the symbols and rites, etc., must be seen in the same context. The president cannot view his intervention in the assembly as the simple unfolding of his personal, charismatic impulses, even if this would enrich the spirituality of the congregation; nor can be regard himself as the organizer of a spectacle open to all who are interested. The president is responsible for seeing that an assembly remains true to itself.

A second rule that follows from this is that the president has to seek communion at every moment. If he is factious or partisan, he will disrupt the community; if he is subjective and inclined to impose his own inspirations, he will become a factor for disintegration, as he will if he makes distinctions between persons, thereby denying the most radical Christian quality: love. At the level of greater hierarchical intervention, a president who fails to integrate the community is seriously defiling the image of Christ the head, whom he is supposed to be representing sacramentally in the midst of the assembly. In practical and positive terms, all this involves acceptance of charisms, promotion of good relationships among the community, distribution of functions so that all can play their part; it also involves paying special attention to the poorer and weaker brethren—the only acceptable distinction between persons—to encourage them to fulfil their potentialities. It means, too, educating the community so that all its members can accept each other, with all their limitations and aspirations....

As a servant of communion, the president is also responsible for the catholicity of an assembly. Here one has to think in physical terms: the more homogeneous a community is, the greater the need for the president to preserve it from sectarianism; the more heterogeneous, the greater the need to make its purpose brazenly clear and to see that the precept of love is fulfilled. This implies knowing how to welcome members who join the community from other places and other cultures, following the tradition of the early Church: "Contribute to the needs of the saints, practise hospitality" (Rom.

12. 13). This is particularly important in this age of constant population mobility. On the other hand, catholicity does not exclude adaptation to a particular liturgical assembly, with all its particularities of language, symbols, etc.: an assembly is always a particular one, happening at a certain time in a certain place; it is never an abstraction. Christians who join an assembly from other places should feel welcomed in faith and love, but they should not expect that assembly to dilute its essence for the (theoretical) sake of greater catholicity; this would result in making it impossible to integrate them into the community, because it would no longer be an entity. This is a delicate task, requiring patience in study and skill in educating people.

Finally, one last rule that affects mainly those who exercise hierarchical mediation: the rule of headship in brotherliness. Each assembly is a gathering of brothers: the "You are all brothers" of Mt. 23. 8 includes the presbyter and the bishop. The hierarchical ministerial function is a brotherly one that can be understood only from inside the assembly, just as hierarchy can be understood only from within the Church. But the minister's brotherly service is to represent Jesus Christ in an active and effective way; it is the sacrament of the Lord in the midst of his brethren gathered together. In practical terms, this cannot mean either a sacralized or "spiritualized" distancing of oneself from the assembly, hardly looking at those present, nor an apologetic attitude, almost hiding behind the altar. . . . The presidency involves making certain gestures and, above all, talking to those present as to friends (cf. Jn. 15. 15), and being in the midst of them as one who serves (Lk. 22. 27).

*　　　*　　　*

I have tried to keep three lines of contemporary ecclesiological thought in mind throughout the preceding commentary: communion as a radical element in the people of God, interpretation of the ministry in terms of service, and fidelity to the identity of the Church. These lines converge spontaneously when the Church is made visible, which is just what happens in liturgical assemblies. We know, in effect, that "this Church of Christ is truly present in all legitimate local congregations . . . united with their pastors" (*Const. on the Church*, 26).

Translated by Paul Burns

Aidan Kavanagh

Ministries in the Community and in the Liturgy

MANY causes contribute to the current crisis of ministerial identity. Surely major among them is an excessively narrow view of ministry. This view has confined the reality of Christian ministry largely to the major ecclesiastical orders, particularly to the episcopacy and presbyterate. The concept and the reality of ministry in the Church have thus become brittle. More seriously, however, much evidence on Christian ministry as a far more diversified structure both from historical sources and contemporary life has, in the narrowing process, been rendered inaudible to ears that need most to hear it. Whole structures of ministry have thus been allowed to atrophy, new possibilities for ministry go unexploited, and the future potential of both for invigorating the Church's mission and self-awareness have not been actualized.

Neither the New Testament nor the main line of subsequent Christian tradition can be blamed for this constriction. It has become standard to note that the main if not exclusive New Testament term for ministry, *diakonia*, is broad and not exclusively ecclesiastical. It is a Greek equivalent of the Aramaic word Jesus, used to designate his own central intention: this, he insisted, must be appropriated in his own followers (Mk. 10. 43–45, and 26–28). Ephesians 4. 9–12, in listing the main ecclesial charisms (apostles, prophets, evangelists, pastors and teachers), specifies further that all these exist "... so that the saints together may be one in the work of ministry (*diakonias*), building up the Body of Christ." This implies that all members of the local community share in *diakonia*.[1] Such ministry might be to physical needs, as when Peter's mother-in-law served those about her after she had been healed by Jesus. The word was used of the women who ministered to the needs of Jesus and the apostles; and it is said that the seven deacons were appointed so that widows in the Jerusalem community might be ministered to without discrimination—perhaps implying also that the apostles might thereby be freed to pursue the apostolic ministry that was uniquely theirs (Acts 6. 1–6). Paul speaks of the gifts to be collected from the Gentile communities as ministering to the needs of the mother church in Jerusalem (2 Cor. 8. 4; 9. 1).

It is clear in the New Testament that the scope of *diakonia* or ministry is nothing less than the whole of Christian life, involving the whole community of faith as one grand "ministry of reconciliation" (2 Cor. 5. 18–20). The New Testament's association between ministry (*diakonia*) and community (*koinonia*) derives, as J. Blenkinsopp notes, "...from the conviction that both are the creation of the Spirit of God now manifest and operative through Christ."[2] According to Paul, Christian ministry is radically one of reconciliation that can only be realized in a newly covenanted and Spirit-filled people (2 Cor. 3. 6; 5. 5). This ministry is God's work entirely: "It was God who reconciled us to himself through Christ and gave us the work of handing on this reconciliation" (2 Cor. 5. 18–19). Crucial in this process is *the word* that must be proclaimed (1 Cor. 1. 17) and heard (Rom. 10. 14). So far from being a purely literary affair, the word as Paul uses it is defined as "power" (1 Cor. 1. 18)—power to save, to convict of sin, to change the human condition. Remove this focal point of Christian *diakonia*, and it collapses into mere good deeds engaged in to alleviate human needs that arise within man's tragic condition but leave that condition basically untouched. Yet man's condition is precisely what Jesus attacked, and to leave it untouched is at best a genial form of disbelief in him. It is also to evacuate Christian ministry of its central content and primary purpose. Alleviation of personal and social needs is surely a part of Christian *diakonia*: however, it is not the substance

---

[1] Cf. Kenneth Scott Latourette, "The Diaconate: Sacred or Outmoded?" in *The Diaconate Now*, ed. Richard T. Nolan (Washington, 1968), p. 171.

[2] *Celibacy, Ministry, Church* (New York, 1968), p. 244.

but one result of the primary ministry which Blenkinsopp calls that of the Word. "Therefore", he continues, "the primary categories are those of speech, sign and language. Jesus' miracles of healing are signs of a new age, a new possibility for man struggling with the questionableness of his existence. The great commissioning at the end of Matthew's gospel speaks of convincing, making disciples, teaching. Paul is above all 'a minister of Christ Jesus in the priestly service of the gospel of God' (Rom. 15. 16)."[3] Thus the number and importance of those charismatic gifts that involve speech and communication—prophetic utterance, teaching, exhortation, tongues and their interpretation.[4] The implication is therefore unavoidable that ministry was regarded at the origin of Christian tradition as having to do with leadership in creating channels of communication for the building up of a community covenanted and Spirit-filled in Christ Jesus.[5]

Against this background the concept of Christian ministry takes on a vital robustness, and the reality of Christian ministry assumes a breadth that often goes undetected in the post-medieval Church. Ministry outside the liturgy and ministry inside the liturgy lose their apparent opposition, an opposition often specified as that between unreal and real. Persons in love, for example, can be seen as consecrated primarily for a crucial ministry that is far broader and more complex than any liturgical ministry. It is a ministry of reconciliation to each other, in their family, and to the world as it immediately impinges upon their discrete sector of life. Yet it would be narrow in the extreme to rule out this ministry's regular manifestation in formal acts of liturgical worship. Spouses minister to each other the sacrament of their union under the criteria of the Gospel in the most formal way; they form their children in faith and repentance, and in the liturgical expression of both most directly; they "concelebrate" their children's initiation into the community of faith, overtly engaging in specific acts of the rite with the presiding minister; they are expected to minister to the poor, the dying,

[3] *Op. cit.*, p. 246.

[4] On teaching as an office in the New Testament, cf. John McKenzie, *Authority in the Church* (New York, 1966), pp. 78–86.

[5] Cf. Blenkinsopp, *op. cit.*, p. 247. On "apostolic leadership", cf. also, McKenzie, *op. cit.*, p. 121.

and to the elderly who come especially within the orbit of their responsibility. Where, in all this, liturgy begins and liturgy leaves off is a question that can be posed only when pathologically narrow views of ministry and liturgy are abroad: the non-occurrence of such questions may well be a sign of health.

The concrete reality of a life in faith is the source of Christian ministry as well as of liturgy: it is also the on-going *Sitz im Leben* of both. Both ultimately are one reality, and that reality is not just life-in-general, but life in Jesus. Granted this, it may be advantageous to look at two separate and quite different historical contexts in which that same life has been lived—to detect contrasts that might shed some light on ministerial structures in our own day. Theories aside, perhaps statistics can speak even more strongly to pastoral problems presently sensed but difficult to define and nearly impossible to solve.

The earliest statistical report on ministerial structure is given by Eusebius for the church of Rome, c. 250.[6] Lietzmann estimates the city's population at this period at about 1,000,000,[7] and others that Christians numbered about 40,000 during the same period.[8] The ratio of Christians to others in Rome would have then been 1:25. That at present between Roman Catholics and the rest of the population in the United States is almost 1:4.

The period was a difficult one for the church of Rome. At least two internal schisms had occurred within the previous thirty years; bishops had resigned, one had been banished, two slain, and the Decian persecution was beginning. During all this, the Bishop of Rome, Cornelius, notes that the formal ministerial structure in the city encompassed

> 1 bishop
> 46 presbyters
> 7 deacons
> 7 subdeacons
> 42 acolytes
> 52 exorcists, readers, and church maintenance
> personnel (*ostiarii*).

[6] Eusebius, *The History of the Church* (Baltimore, 1965), p. 282 [Bk. 6. 43].
[7] H. Lietzmann, *A History of the Early Church*, Vol. 1 (New York,[3] 1963), p. 239.
[8] Williamson in Eusebius, *op. cit.*, p. 282.

In addition, on the rolls as formal recipients of charity (probably amounting to total or near-total support) were 1500 "widows and distressed [ill] persons".[9]

These statistics may not appear very significant. But they do become interesting in their ratios, especially when those ratios are compared on the same basis with the ministerial statistics of 1970 for the Roman Catholic community in the United States. The statistics of 1 bishop for 40,000 faithful in A.D. 250 translates to over 1200 bishops for the Catholic population in the United States—four times the present number of bishops (295), and almost eight times the number of bishops who are heads of local churches (161). Yet the ratio of presbyters to people is slightly lower in third-century Rome (1:956) than today in the United States (1:831). To equal the number of deacons attached to a bishop then would require almost 8,500 deacons (plus an equal number of subdeacons) now in the United States, functioning as a permanent non-presidential major order with regular pastoral and administrative duties.

So far as the minor orders are concerned, the total of 94 in third-century Rome would mean over 113,000 in the United States today (an average of about 700 persons in each of the 161 dioceses), persons who devote at least part of their time *ex professo* to the act of worship and to charity, either directly or indirectly.

The number of formal recipients of charity in Rome at Cornelius' time may not seem large—only 1500 out of a church membership of 40,000 and a total urban population of 1 million. But such an undertaking in the Catholic community in the United States today would mean giving total or nearly total support to 1.8 million people. Basing the cost of this on a sub-poverty grant of $2,000 per person each year would mean an outlay of no less than $3.6 billion annually.

Although the statistics from third-century Rome are admittedly conjectural to some extent (except for the actual numbers of ministers mentioned by Cornelius), the variance in ratios between ministers and people then and now in the United States cannot be overlooked. The variance reveals quite different ministerial profiles

[9] *Ibid.*

in the ratios of bishops to people. Quadrupling the number
of American bishops, or multiplying the number of American
dioceses by eight times, is a suggestion that will probably not
soon be made: yet doing this might be one way of putting effective pastoral action within range of the episcopacy. Presently
there are far too few bishops and slightly too many presbyters—
at least according to the pattern of pre-Constantinian Rome.
The American church is not so much an episcopal as a presbyteral
one, according to this pattern. The current ratio of bishops to
presbyters (1:194 now versus 1:46 in Rome) and of bishops to
people (1:160,600 now versus 1:40,000 in Rome) may afford
some insight into why unfortunate modifications in ecclesial
polity and sacramental practice have occurred: their having come
to be accepted as normal may account for the exasperating
pastoral inefficiency one encounters on the highest ministerial
levels—an inefficiency due less to poor intentions than to sheer
social dynamics.

To be explicit, if there is a ratio of only one bishop for every
194 presbyters and every 160,600 laity, what does it really mean
on the pastoral level to speak of Christian worship, as the Constitution on the Sacred Liturgy (para. 26) does, as "...a holy
people united and organized under their bishops"? Episcopal
presence in the acts of a local church's worship is the exception,
not the rule. Those main liturgical acts still reserved to the bishop
—confirmation, ordination and the blessing of chrism—have
become, moreover, precisely the liturgical acts most infrequently
participated in by all, and the acts least and worst understood as
a result. Other episcopal liturgies such as the public reconciliation of penitents, the consecration of dedicated women religious,
and the blessing of abbots—not to say episcopal presidency at
celebrations of the Divine Office—for all practical purposes have
ceased to contribute in the formation of the Church's liturgical
piety. For the most part, when a modern bishop functions liturgically he does so as a presbyter, a senior presbyter at best. The
Western Church has in fact grown so accustomed to presbyteral
ministry that it feels either uncomfortable or unsure with any
other form of ministry. In third-century Rome there was a highly
diversified ministerial structure (implying equally diversified
exercise of charisms) involving 155 persons within a community

of some 40,000—a ratio of one minister for every 26 people. In the United States in 1970 there was a fairly undiversified ministerial structure far and away sustained by some 60,000 presbyters within a community of almost 50 million—a ratio of one presbyter for every 800 people.

Without passing value judgments on ministerial quality, it is little wonder that, according to the norms of social dynamics, the episcopacy has become increasingly problematic; that ministries other than the presbyteral are in eclipse; and that pastoral endeavour is either sporadic, or inadequate, or both. The ministerial structure that has developed in the Western Church is the main social factor reinforcing an unacceptably narrow view of Christian *diakonia*. When one speaks of church ministry, it is normal that the operative paradigm is a presbyteral one. For this reason, one might suggest, no categories or vocabulary for other sorts of publicly recognizable formal ministries can emerge. True ministries indeed exist all the while, e.g., those of service to the ill in hospitals, to certain of the poor, to prisoners, and above all to the young in schools and to the unconverted in missions. But there is hardly any way such true ministries might be recognized as being formally *within* the ministerial structure rather than being only materially and extrinsically attached to it.

This factor has hampered not only pastoral efforts, but fundamental reflection on the nature and scope of the Church itself. More specific to the concerns of this article, the same factor has inhibited the diversification of formal liturgical roles other than the presidential ones of bishop and presbyter. What have come to be called the minor orders have lapsed into curiosities enshrined within seminary walls. Outside seminaries these orders have been farced by such activities as the induction of altar boys into organizations like the "Knights of the Altar", and the more recent "commissionings" of lay readers and commentators. Why such contributions of services should not be regarded as true ministries within and for local churches, and why they should not receive formal recognition by liturgical inclusion into the "orders" or groups dedicated to their practice, are questions unanswerable except in terms of the restriction of formal ministry to presidential roles described above.

The same sort of difficulty pertains also to the non-presidential role of the deacon.[10] It is curious to note in many of the recent discussions on restoring the diaconate as a permanent order in the Roman Rite a tendency to expect in the candidate for such an office what once were mainly presbyteral characteristics—older age, mature judgment, accomplishment in life, and even allowance in some cases that such a one might be married and have a family. Of serious concern in all this is whether, so long as the presbyteral paradigm of ministry remains supported by a largely undifferentiated ministerial structure and assumptions, deacons of this description will be generally accepted and adequately made use of. How, for example, will such a deacon relate to a group of presbyters younger, less mature and experienced than he; and how will this relationship be construed by the rank and file of the people? Much potential good stands to result from the re-establishment of a permanent diaconate in the Roman Rite—so much good, in fact, that its possible failure due to merely ordaining such men *without a concomitant alteration in ministerial structure so as adequately to accommodate their order* is cause for concern. It is urgent that the question of permanent diaconal ministry not be obscured by tertiary concerns touching marital status or sex of the candidate. As emotion-laden and interesting as these questions may be, they are far less crucial than those of what a deacon is and what a deacon *as such* can do that no one else can or should do in the ministry of reconciliation. If the nature and function of the non-presidential role of the deacon in the general ministry of the Church is not given clear practical articulation, it will be even more difficult to do the same so far as other non-presidential ministries are concerned. And if neither is done, a richer understanding of the Church as servant—a ministerial ecclesiology—will have suffered serious inhibition.

The point is a major one and deserves further comment. So long as the present conventional situation of a largely undifferentiated ministry centred on the presbyterate remains in force, there is little the Western Church can do pastorally, theologically, and liturgically but to go on doing the same as now. We shall, by ordaining numbers of deacons out of training programmes already in operation, run a high risk of creating a group of

---

[10] Cf. K. Rahner and H. Vorgrimler (eds.), *Diaconia in Christo* [*Quaestiones Disputatae* 15/16] (Freiburg, 1962).

superannuated Knights of the Altar without pastoral effectiveness, liturgical necessity, or theological importance. This will simply repeat a tendency already in evidence since the recent Council— that of undertaking reforms in isolation from all else and without intelligent reflecting before the fact on what such reforms require to keep from faltering. The result of such faltering is disillusionment at best and ennui in faith at worst. With only good intentions taking the place of insight, the ministry of reconciliation may slide into a ministry of division with alarming ease. This is not to imply that nothing should be done. It is to insist that doing anything about a problem is no substitute for doing something at the problem's heart.

The heart of the problem is not directly touched by instituting training programmes for deacons. It is touched even less by the sort of simplification of minor orders recently announced in the press—a programme designed, according to reports, to clarify the "step towards the priesthood". The present anachronistic formalities of the minor orders surely need attention, but the fundamental reason for their existence is at least recognition of the need for ministerial diversity in the Church rather than as first steps to the presbyterate. Again, the assumption in the reform of minor orders apparently centres on the presbyteral paradigm of ministry. The exorcist as one who possesses in some visible measure the gift of healing; the acolyte as one who possesses in some visible measure the gift of assisting splendidly in the act of worship; the "door keeper" as one who is remarkable in his or her devotion to the care of the places in which the community of faith meets for worship; the reader as one able to announce the word publicly and with sensitivity (a quality that seems to grow more rare as literacy increases); the catechist who can teach the faith superbly; the confessor who can counsel adequately those burdened by sin—all these possess charisms of indispensable service to the Church. Their recognition, by public prayer and induction into recognized groups or "orders" of their peers, seems not only advisable but necessary for an adequate structural statement of the pastoral-theological nature of the ministry of reconciliation typical to the Christian community.

To exercise such gifts *de facto* is one thing; but to receive *de jure* recognition for them and to wield them corporately is to increase their potential and to present a firm basis for an expansion of insight into the very nature of ministry—and through this into the full reality of the Church as an *institution* shot through with grace and mystery. No amount of theorizing on charisms, and not even the unrecognized exercise of such gifts, will suffice to secure the benefits that can accrue from giving visible public structure to their reality within the Church. There is no other way to account for their emergence as ministerial orders in the pre-Constantinian Church—a Church obsessed with scriptural warranty and with what was understood to be an authentically apostolic derivation of all ecclesiastical practice. Jesus was not known to have commanded a diaconate; yet he said much about service, *diakonia*. He said nothing about the minor orders either; yet he healed many, proclaimed the word, taught men how to pray, counselled the sinner, cherished the temple enough to cleanse it, and served his Father's will magnificently in the *leiturgia* of his passion. What he did uniquely, whole orders of persons within his Body, the Church, were to do corporately and in concert.

It appears idle to expect significant insight into the Church as ministry until significant diversification of its own ministries comes about. This will bring with it new tensions as yet unknown, to be sure; but it is in such tensions that the most creative moments of historic Catholicism have always originated. The tensions consequent on ministerial diversification would, moreover, not represent elements unknown in the tradition of the Church. Indeed, it is solidly of the tradition that ecclesiastical ministries be so diversified—because Christian life in a community of faith, when lived to its fullest, requires a rich and recognizable diversity of ministerial witness to remain authentic to itself in its mission to the world. There is nothing more novel, in this view, than an undifferentiated ministry centring almost wholly upon the presbyterate as paradigm. When this happens, it makes it impossible to discuss other ministerial charisms as much else than unessential adjuncts to ministry in the essential and "proper" sense at best, or as threats to such ministry at worst. The result is to put whole areas of perception out of range for bishops and presbyters, and whole areas of action beyond the reach of those who do not belong to these orders. This amounts to a drastic constraint on the scope of the Church's mission of service and to a radical reduction in the ways in which the Church itself may be understood. This state of things is unwarranted in tradition itself, as most recently expressed in the Vatican Council's dogmatic constitution on the Church, *Lumen Gentium*, and in its pastoral constitution on the Church in the modern world, *Gaudium et Spes.* It is difficult to imagine how the directions given to the Church's total ministry of reconciliation by the Council can be executed without a ministerial structure much more diversified than at present.

True creativity in this matter, deriving from tradition, might well be directed towards practical ways in which *de facto* exercise of ministerial gifts could be, with prior catechesis, established *de jure* as both restored and newly formed orders of service in the Church. Orders, for example, such as those of catechists, healers, liturgical readers, keepers of churches, workers among the poor and ill, and of widows or others who work with the aged (a group of rapidly growing size in technologized nations). Such orders might be full- or part-time in terms of service; they might also be for contractually stated periods of service as well. Co-ordination of such orders' service may also be the main duty of the reinstituted permanent order of deacons, a duty wholly in keeping with one aspect of tradition's understanding of diaconal ministry.

Perhaps even more important than this, however, such formal ministerial diversification may lead to a richer and more balanced understanding of the offices of bishop and presbyter in the Church. It is possible to argue that at present the presbyterate has become in fact a diaconate in all but name—an unusual diaconate bearing the privileges of presiding at the Eucharist and of reconciling penitents. In this light, those who appear most recognizably in the role of the traditional presbyter are non-diocesan or auxiliary bishops, protonotaries apostolic, and vicars general, whatever their order. It is thus understandable that presbyters today experience identity crises.

Ministerial diversification may aid not only in clarifying the warp in understanding and function of the major orders, however: it may also help the Church see the estate of Christian marriage more clearly as a true order of ministry within the community. The emergence of such an awareness would be most welcome at a time when the family is undergoing a socio-cultural strain that some would call terminal. Yet the many studies in child psychology by Erik Erikson make it clear that ritual, and thus social, formation is borne in the primary and most profound degree by parents—a position repeated recently from an anthropological and linguistic viewpoint by Mary Douglas.[11] No other order, major or minor, can substitute for the ministry of Christian parents in the faith-formation of children. One suspects, however, that this ministry is the one most rapidly declining in effectiveness in the contemporary Church—under grave socio-cultural stress and, unfortunately, all too often with the unintended connivance of official church ministries which view marriage largely as a problem of sexual ethics. The rapid deritualization of family life in modern Western society is an alarming prognosis for liturgical aphasia in the future: and an inability to engage in ritual worship is a radical impediment to social incorporation within a community of faith.

*   *   *

To flatten ecclesiastical ministry out into only one paradigm is to inhibit the scope of Christian ministry and, thus, the Church's mission of critical reconciliation. Analogous to this is the flattening out of liturgical experience into the one paradigm of the Eucharist alone. The orders of episcopacy and presbyterate were not meant to function alone any more than the Eucharist was meant to provide every experience of worship a Christian community must possess in order to remain faithful. Christian life under the Gospel lived in this world is too rich and multiform in both its needs and purposes to function adequately without diversity of ministerial and liturgical structures. These structures, meshed together as they are meant to be, do not exhaust the whole reality of the Church; but they form the central, structural core of the Church's fabric. Diminution of one means not only the diminution of the other; diminution of both means an unacceptable

[11] Cf. Erik Erikson, "The Development of Ritualization," in *The Religious Situation 1968* (Boston, 1968), pp. 711-733; Mary Douglas, *Natural Symbols: Explorations in Cosmology* (New York, 1970), pp. 1-36.

inhibition of the Church itself, the constriction of a radical service the world cannot do without.

Discussion of extensive diversification in ecclesiastical ministries is in this respect an important, if modest, contribution to the good estate of the world itself. The foregoing observations and suggestions are intended to contribute toward this end.

René van Eyden

The Place of Women
in Liturgical Functions

IN Ottawa, April 1971, a conference of bishops coincided with a meeting of Catholic women and the opportunity was taken to ask the bishops to do five things: "(1) To declare clearly and unequivocally that women are full and equal members of the Church, with the same rights, privileges and responsibilities as men; (2) to make strong and immediate representations to the forthcoming synod of bishops, asking that all discriminatory barriers in canon law and tradition be removed; (3) to ordain qualified women for the ministry; (4) by whatever means deemed appropriate, to encourage the presence of qualified women on all bodies dealing with matters which concern all church members; (5) to take all practical measures to ensure that the attitude of the clergy towards women, sexuality and marriage respect the inherent dignity of women."

With the single exception of the auxiliary bishop of the Ukrainian Eparchy of Toronto, who thought that the woman's place was in the home,[1] all the bishops accepted these recommendations and were ready to raise the question of the repeal of discriminatory laws at the 1971 synod. This is only one example in the world of the growing dissatisfaction of women with their subordinate place in the Church.

The Church's new understanding of itself, expressed so clearly at Vatican II, has led to many striking liturgical reforms. In one important respect, however, the liturgy has remained

[1] *National Catholic Reporter*, 30 April 1971, p. 19.

unchanged. It is still essentially dominated by men. The fact that women are even now not permitted to share in many liturgical functions is still not sufficiently recognized.

In every period of the Church's history, the way in which liturgical functions have been distributed and carried out has always reflected the Church's current view of itself. The very fact that women have never been able to exercise any function in the liturgy points to an image of the Church that can no longer be legitimate since the Second Vatican Council's concept of the people of God as consisting of men and women—now women clearly *must* be able to share in liturgical functions.

What has above all to be taken into account is the changing role of woman in society as a whole. The Church, as a social institution, is part of human society and has to develop as that society develops. If new relationships are coming about in human society between man and woman, this may be an indication that new forms of collaboration should also be evolved in the Church and especially in the liturgy.

In the first section of this article, I shall try to show how the roles of the woman and of the man are developing in society. In the second part, I shall discuss the traditional views and legal enactments that prevent women from assuming full responsibility in the Church and the liturgy, and I shall conclude by pointing to various possible ways in which they may be encouraged to play a fuller part.

I. Towards an Equal Position in Society

The First Emancipation

As John XXIII pointed out in *Pacem in Terris*, "woman is taking her place in public life. This process is perhaps quicker in the case of peoples with a Christian civilization and slower in the case of those with other traditions. . . . Woman is becoming more and more conscious of her human dignity. She will therefore no longer be regarded as a soulless being or a tool, but is demanding the full rights of a human person, both in the family and in society. . . . We are at present witnessing the disappearance of age-old views which have led in the case of certain groups of people to an inferiority complex and in the case of others to a

superiority complex, on the basis of socio-economic factors, sex
or the political situation" (*Pacem in Terris*, 41, 43, 1963). Apart
from minor fluctuations, woman has for centuries always been
in the second rank of human society. It is only in the present
century that there has been any radical change. Indeed, the rapid
development of the personal and social position of woman is
perhaps the most important of all the many humanizing movements that are now taking place. Every new step towards freedom taken by woman marks an increase not only in her own
well-being, but in that of man and the whole of society, which
is, after all, based on man-woman relationships.

Recognition of the equal status of woman has come about in
many ways. In many countries, legal equality has been achieved.
Women have obtained the right to vote. Full education is available to girls. Women can exercise public functions and have full
access to work outside the home. The wife is an equal partner in
marriage and the family; in many countries, the law defining
the husband as the "head of the family" has been annulled. The
most important recent change brought about in the life of woman
in society has resulted from the power she now enjoys to regulate
conception. For the first time in history, she is no longer the
victim of successive pregnancies over which she has little control,
with all the lack of freedom and social consequences that this
entails.

Despite this impressive progress, of course, inequality still per-
sists and equal status is still resisted in many places. In some countries, female emancipation has not even begun. In 1967, the
United Nations appealed very strongly to all States to put an end
to all forms of discrimination against women.[2]

The Second Emancipation

This first emancipation, which broadly speaking took the form
of an active struggle by women themselves to obtain equal legal
status within the existing social order, seems now to have come
to an end, and a second phase of fundamentally critical emancipation has begun. This has been marked above all by a wave of

[2] *Declaration on the Elimination of Discrimination against Women*, 7
November 1967.

publications,[3] and by the emergence of action groups concerned with women's liberation in a new society. The legal emancipation already achieved is now seen to be no more than a beginning. Women have, formally and legally, equal rights, but they do not, for example, enjoy equal pay for all equal work and equal opportunities even if they are equally well qualified. Girls have fewer opportunities than boys of the same social background. The old ideas about the place of women in society still persist, with the result that women still often feel professionally insecure about their identity as women.

During the first phase, women tried to obtain the status of men within the existing structures of society. Now, however, they are looking for emancipation within a changed society, because the unequal status of women is perpetuated by the existing institutions. Man, too, is seen to be the victim of social expectations which restrict his freedom. An example of this is resistance to men in the social services and to women in administration. The demand that is now being made is that suitability and ambition, not sex, should be the criteria for the distribution of social functions. The developments leading to a radical change in the roles of man and woman are described in a report submitted to U.N.O. by the Swedish government in 1968:[4] man and woman are equal partners and either or both can perform a family role or a professional function, but if this is to be achieved, many social provisions and changes in the traditional social institutions have to be made. The emancipation of woman is seen to be very closely associated with that of man.

A striking feature of this second emancipation is the increasingly important part played in it by a radical criticism of society itself. The prevailing powers in modern technocratic society are anonymous, and these constitute a threat to human freedom. A real liberation of both man and woman can only be achieved if society as a whole is renewed: if authoritarian structures are made more democratic and education is remodelled so that boys and girls grow up in a new relationship with each other.

[3] See, for example, Kate Millett, *Sexual Politics* (New York, 1970); Sara Doely, ed., *Women's Liberation and the Church* (New York, 1970).
[4] *The Status of Women in Sweden* (Report to the United Nations: Stockholm, 1968).

There is also the Marxist view that only revolution can free
women from their oppression, which is only an aspect of the
total oppression of the proletariat by the capitalist system; and
that the solidarity of working-class men and women together
must consequently be greater than that of all women of all
classes.[5] This view has made the women who belong to modern
action groups more aware of the connection between the oppression of women and the capitalist system, but they are rightly re-
luctant to reduce their problem to the level of a mere aspect of
the class struggle. They do not believe that the creation of a Com-
munist society will automatically do away with discrimination
against their sex.

Of the many women's action groups in the world today—with
their different answers to the question, "Must the struggle for
emancipation be conducted with, without or against men?"—
the most influential and rapidly expanding is the American
Women's Liberation Movement,[6] which is "simply organized
anger against real oppression".[7] All the members of this movement are women, who insist that, like Negroes, they are almost
always given second place in all militant left-wing groups as in
society as a whole.

We may, however, conclude that the problem of man is as
acute as that of woman in a society in which men are dominant.
As David Jenkins, the Director of Human Studies (World Council of Churches), has said: "How dehumanizing is this male
domination? And this is a question not only about the opportunities women have for being human but also about the de-
humanization of men. For oppression dehumanizes the oppressor
even more than it dehumanizes the oppressed."[8]

---

[5] See Karin Schrader-Klebert, "Die kulturelle Revolution der Frau", in
Kursbuch 17 (1969); Juliet Mitchel, "Women. The Longest Revolution",
in New Left Review 40 (November 1966).

[6] Notes from the Second Year: Women's Liberation. Major Writings of
the Radical Feminists (New York, 1970).

[7] Risk, Vol. 7, No. 1: "Gladly We Rebel" (Education and Communication of the WCC), p. 53. The terms "oppression" and "liberation" point
to the revolutionary seriousness of this new consciousness of discrimination against women.

[8] David E. Jenkins, "Towards One New Man in Jesus Christ" (Address
to the Central Commission of the WCC; Addis Ababa, January 1971).

II. Women in the Liturgy of the People of God

The Vatican Council recognized that the Church had to turn towards the world and to collaborate in the dialogue with man about his future. (The task of the Church is, for example, "to examine the signs of the times and to interpret them in the light of the Gospel", *Gaudium et Spes*, 4.) If this is so, then it is not difficult to see the emancipation of women as a genuine human process and a fulfilment of evangelical teaching, since, as M.-D. Chenu has said, "the Gospel comes to us with all its contemporary message in the questions asked by our contemporaries".[9]

The Church is committed, by its very nature, to be a community in which equality is visibly present. Yet, throughout history, the ideal man-woman relationship has seldom been realized in the Church, which has consequently suffered from a great impoverishment as a community led exclusively by men, and as one lacking the contribution that could have been made by women. Contemporary woman's struggle for equality and a fuller life as a human being may be a clear "sign of the times" and an appeal to the Church to find a Christian, humane solution.

I should like now to discuss very briefly the causes of the very small part that women have played in the Church's liturgy up to the present and at the same time the traditional position of woman in the Church, because the two are very closely connected.

1. *The Traditional Place of Woman*

The freedom that woman has already achieved in society as a whole has been largely in spite of rather than thanks to the Church.[10] The ideas and practices of the Church emerge from any analysis of social mechanisms as powerful factors in the preservation of female inequality: "As a hierarchically organized social structure, the Church has played an important part in reinforcing discrimination against women, ensuring that taboos and value judgments have been given a religious sanction and that all transgression of the rules of society has been punished."[11] The

[9] M.-D. Chenu, "De tekenen des tijds", in *De Kerk in de wereld van deze tijd* (Hilversum, 1967), pp. 55–77, especially p. 77.

[10] Mary Daly, *The Church and the Second Sex* (New York, 1968).

[11] *Kirche 1985* (working paper No. 8 of the Swiss Institute of Pastoral Sociology, 1971), p. 130.

Church's attitude to women has been conditioned by that of the society of which it has formed a part, but the reverse is also true—the teaching and the life of the Church have also influenced the position accorded to woman in society. The Church has regarded the prevailing order in society, in which woman is subordinate to man, as willed by God and as something that no man may change. As a result, the Church has consistently stood in the way of all progress.

Despite the fact that important work has been done by women, especially nuns, in the Church (teaching, nursing, missionary work, etc.), they have played a very small part in specifically ecclesiastical functions (preaching, pastoral work and the liturgy). Their exclusion from liturgical functions, however, does not date from the origin of the Church, but is the result of later developments in history.

Women had at least two offices in the early Church. They functioned as widows and as deaconesses (see 1 Tim. 5. 9; Rom. 16. 1), with duties—because there was still no uniform codification—which varied according to time and place. Generally speaking, the duties of the widow were charitable and pastoral, whereas those of the deaconess were mainly liturgical. These included the care of the sick and the poor, instructing women in the faith and helping to baptize them, bringing communion to them and children, and leading in prayer, singing and readings from Scripture. Women were ordained as deaconesses in the same way as men were ordained as deacons—by the bishop's imposition of hands and prayer in the presence of others holding office as priest, deacon or deaconess. In the East (Constantinople), deaconesses received the stole and communion under both kinds after the imposition of hands. In the *Didascalia* (Syria, middle of the third century), we read: "You must honour the deaconess as the image of the Holy Spirit" (the deacon as the image of Christ).

There are various reasons for the gradual disappearance of women's offices in the Church. Firstly, there was the increasing centralization of power in the figure of the bishop and the increasing emphasis placed on the hierarchy, the male members of which assumed more and more authority. Women in office in the Church were the first victims of this. Secondly, from the beginning of the third century onwards, the person of the minister and his liturgical actions came to be regarded as sacral, the imposition of hands to be thought of as a consecration, and the minister of the word to be called a priest, a minister of the sacrifice of the altar.[12] Since sexuality was thought to be unclean and improper in this sacral sphere, the priest had to be unmarried and women were excluded from sacral functions because of their periodic cultic uncleanness. The ordination of deaconesses was forbidden by councils and synods. Thirdly, the rise of monastic life and the growing appreciation of virginity led to a gradual movement of deaconesses away from the community and into convents. Fourthly, the important part played by women in sects, as priests or bishops, and the excesses committed in such circles brought the office of women into discredit. Finally, and perhaps most important of all, in contradiction to the attitude towards women displayed by the Christ of the gospels, many of the Church Fathers described women as inferior beings. Gnostic ideas about the body and sexuality crept into Christian teaching and led to a denigration of women,[13] who were banned from church functions, given second place in the life of the Church and were even subjected to humiliating laws (such as the ban imposed by the Council of Auxerre in 578 on the reception of the eucharistic bread by women in their bare hands, to prevent pollution).

The arguments put forward by the Church Fathers and the Councils were handed down without question from century to century, with the result that this view of woman came to be accepted as the Christian view. This theory and practice were concretely reflected in the laws of the Church and many are still embodied in the *Codex Iuris Canonici*,[14] which not only includes a number of discriminatory articles, but also bears the unmistakable imprint of a man-centred view of humanity. Among the laws relating to the liturgy are those which state that a woman is not permitted to serve at mass and that only a man can be ordained.

[12] G. Siefer, "Der Priester ein geweihter Mann?", in *Diakonia* 4 (1969), pp. 35 52, 106–13; J. P. Audet, *Mariage et célibat dans le service pastoral de l'Eglise* (Paris, 1967), pp. 117–37.

[13] J. Blank, "Abbau kultischer Sexualtabus und überholter Machtstrukturen", in *Diakonia* 2 (1971), pp. 105–9.

[14] Ida Raming, *Zum Ausschluss der Frau vom Amt in der Kirche* (Münster, 1970).

What is more, because all liturgical texts were composed by men,[15] the spirit and language of the liturgy were as essentially masculine as the practice of the liturgy in Christian communities. (For example, God was addressed as "he" and the concept of God—the Father, Son and Holy Spirit—was masculine.) This led to a reinforcement of male superiority, in no way mitigated by the increasingly explicit attention paid to Mary. The liturgical models of sanctity were overwhelmingly male.[16] (Only twenty per cent of the canonized saints have been women.) Finally, side by side with this very subordinate place accorded to women in concrete life has been the excessive glorification of the romantic ideal of woman.[17]

2. *The Signs of a Change since Vatican II*

Several of the conciliar documents include passages which reveal a new attitude in the Church towards women, but by far the most promising sign for the future is the Church's new understanding of itself as the people of God. The rediscovery of this biblical concept is at the same time a recognition of the equality of all believers in the fundamental dignity of being Christians. It also includes a recognition of the priesthood of all believers, that all are called and sent by Christ to take his Gospel in word and deed out into the world. All believers receive the same Holy Spirit, who gives his grace to all for the well-being of the whole community.

As far as the liturgy is concerned, what is important in the re-emergence of this ancient conviction is that the "Church" is, as it was in early Christianity, primarily the local worshipping community in which the word is proclaimed and the Eucharist celebrated together in the service of the world. The congregation as

---

[15] A. Zarri, "Woman's Prayer and Man's Liturgy", in *Concilium*, Vol. 2 (1970), pp. 73–86 (American edn., Vol. 52).

[16] P. Delooz, *Sociologie et Canonisations* (Liège and The Hague, 1969), p. 261.

[17] Recent examples of this are Pope Paul VI's idealization of woman in his address to Italian gynaecologists on 29 October 1966 and in his homily of 29 September 1970, when he raised Teresa of Avila to the rank of a doctor of the Church (a homily in which he also referred to Paul's text, 1 Cor. 14. 34, saying that this still meant that no woman can ever occupy the hierarchical office of teacher or priest in the Church. This exegesis caused some surprise among theologians.)

a whole is the subject of the liturgy and their priest is there to lead them in worship, to interpret their liturgy and to symbolize their unity with the other local communities.

This means that the liturgy and the life of the Church are open to far greater pluriformity. When the liturgy is really in tune with man's contemporary social environment, that is, in Europe and America at least with a society in which women are emancipated, then more and more opportunities are bound to exist for women to take a leading part in liturgical functions.

The real achievement of Vatican II, then, has been this better climate of thought, rather than any of the resulting texts of the new liturgy. This does not mean that there have been no improvements at all as far as women are concerned. The earlier blessing of the bride in the marriage service has, for example, been replaced by a blessing of the bride and bridegroom (*Ordo celebrandi matrimonium*, 120) and the baptismal rite includes a concluding prayer for the child's mother and father (*Ordo baptismi parvulorum*, 70 and 105). On the other hand, the "Third Instruction for the Correct Application of the Constitution on the Sacred Liturgy" (5 September 1970) is disappointing: "According to the traditional liturgical directions of the Church, it is forbidden for women (girls, married women or religious) to serve the priest at the altar in church, at home, in a convent, college or women's institute." Women are, however, allowed to read the lessons, though not the gospel, and the bidding prayers and to lead the singing. In various countries, women already act as acolytes and readers in the celebration of the Eucharist. Permission has been given in some dioceses for lay men and women to help in the distribution of communion and to receive communion in the hands. The earlier idea that the bread and the cup could not be touched by lay people has in this way been quietly removed, together with the "metaphysical iconostasis" which stood for so long between lay people and the Eucharist.

In spite of these improvements, however, the Church's new self-understanding cannot be consistently put into practice until the problem of women in the liturgy and in the Church's office is openly faced. For the first time in the history of the Church, the question of admitting women officially to office in the Church was discussed publicly in 1970, when the following recommendation was made to the Pastoral Council of the Dutch Church: "It is advisable that as soon as possible women should be further admitted to all ecclesial tasks to which their appointment is not (or hardly) a problem. Further development should be directed towards their being able to fulfil all ecclesiastical functions, not excluding presiding over the Eucharist."[18]

The importance of this question is becoming more and more apparent—no longer as a merely theoretical problem, but as a task calling for a practical answer. Resolutions have been made at a number of international congresses demanding an equal place for women in the Church and requesting that serious consideration be given to the question of women in the Church's office.[19] Renewed theological thinking since Vatican II about the whole question of office in the Church and different ways of carrying out that office in practice should do much to encourage the acceptance of women as office-bearers in the Church. The older conception of office as purely cultic has given way to a view which emphasizes the prophetic and proclamatory aspects of office. The principle of collegiality has been stressed repeatedly and the office of deacon for married men has been reintroduced. Other renewals have included increased differentiation in official tasks, new forms of pastoral teamwork, a "declericalization" of the college of office-bearers and the possibility of married as well as unmarried priests. Within the total framework of these far-reaching renewals, there is a real possibility that women may be called to the office of deacon or priest.

As many exegetes and dogmatic theologians have pointed out, there is no convincing theological reason why women should not be given office in the Church.[20] Non-theological factors, however, play a very important part in excluding women from office. According to Gregory Baum, a distinction must be made in the Church between the *fides catholica* and "Catholic ideology". The

---

[18] Report of the Pastoral Council of the Dutch Province of the Church (January 1970), p. 330.

[19] Third World Congress for the Lay Apostolate (1967); St Joan's International Alliance (1968); World Union of Catholic Women's Organizations (1969); International Theologians' Congress of *Concilium* (1970); European Priests' Conference (1971).

[20] See, for example, H. van der Meer, *Priestertum der Frau?* (Freiburg, 1969) and Ida Raming, *op. cit.*

LIBRARY
KENRICK SEMINARY
7800 KENRICK ROAD
ST. LOUIS, MISSOURI 63119

way in which the Gospel is presented, Baum believes, is often a subtle defence of the ecclesiastical system, personal power, social privilege and group superiority.[21] Resistance to the acceptance of women as office-bearers is often connected with an authoritarian structure, two of the main characteristics of which are a tendency to see woman as a totally different being and a complete inability to endure the presence of woman as an equal.[22] A great deal of resistance is also the result of a hierarchical view of human society as a whole and in the Church in particular. This view, according to which mankind is graded in a scale of superiority and inferiority, not arbitrarily or because of social circumstances, but by virtue of the nature and being of man in a cosmos ordered by God, is still very prevalent in the Church.[23] In this hierarchical structure, woman is, by her very nature, subordinate to man in the family, the Church and society. The priest, on the other hand, as the man who offers sacrifices and mediates between God and men, is the exponent *par excellence* of the sacral scale of values and of man's inherent superiority. Only men can therefore be priests, and the exclusion of women from the priesthood is based on the natural law.

At the Vatican Council, the Catholic Church showed a deep appreciation of the other Christian Churches and it is therefore clear that they may inspire it to renewal, especially in the matter of the admission of women to offices and services in the Church. What the other Churches regard as a blessing and an enrichment can hardly be regarded as impossible by the Catholic Church. A statement was made by the Anglican Churches at the 1968 Lambeth Conference "that those made deaconesses by laying on of hands with appropriate prayers be declared to be within the diaconate".[24] In February 1971, the Anglican Consultative Council passed a resolution "that if he (a bishop) decides to

[21] Gregory Baum, "De toekomst van de kerk", in Report of the International Congress of *Concilium*, Brussels, 1970.

[22] E. Nadler and W. Morrow, "Authoritarian Attitudes toward Women and their Correlates", in *The Journal of Social Psychology* 49 (1959), pp. 113–23.

[23] E. Gössmann, "Women as Priests?", in *Concilium*, Vol. 4 (1968), pp. 59–64 (American edn., Vol. 34).

[24] *The Lambeth Conference, 1968. Resolutions and Reports* (London, 1968), p. 39.

ordain women to the priesthood, his action will be acceptable to this Council; and that this Council will use its good offices to encourage all Provinces of the Anglican Communion to continue in communion with these dioceses".[25] The World Council of Churches held a consultation "On the Ordination of Women" in September 1970. One of the findings of this consultation was that discrimination, connected with the system prevailing in the Church, still often persisted in those churches admitting women to office. In many churches, therefore, it was necessary to investigate the underlying suppositions of this system, and R. W. Henderson is of the opinion that "ordination of women may be seen as a test case in the on-going process of the Church learning to trust the Holy Spirit".[26]

Even in the Catholic Church, the way has already been prepared for the admission of women to office in the Church by the fact that they are already functioning in liturgical and pastoral tasks. For a number of years, for example, in Brazil, Porto Rico and Venezuela, nuns have been leading in services of the word, and have been preaching, baptizing, conducting funerals and distributing communion whenever it has not been possible for a priest to be present.[27] Women have been acting as official ministers, with the approval of bishops and the people, in diaspora situations and in territories where there have been insufficient priests. A number of official functions have been taken over by non-priests—men and women, married and unmarried persons —in other countries as well.

There is, however, still a great deal of uneasiness among some Christians about, and resistance to, women in liturgical functions. Many of their objections are, of course, emotional and disappear as soon as they are able to see for themselves how well women perform these functions. The best way to prepare women to play their part in the liturgy is to enable them to function together with others in various forms of pastoral teamwork. Before this can be

[25] *The Time is Now. Anglican Consultative Council. First Meeting* (London, 1971), p. 39.
[26] R. W. Henderson, "Reflections on the Ordination of Women", in *Study Encounter* 7 (1971), pp. 1-6, especially p. 6; Elsie Gibson, *When the Minister is a Woman* (New York, 1970).
[27] *Informations Catholiques Internationales*, 4, No. 5 (1 March 1970).

done, however, they must have received sufficient training up to the required level. This means that girls must be encouraged to study theology and more opportunities must be provided for pastoral training. The church authorities should have an effective policy for recruiting female candidates by offering real prospects of appointment to offices in the Church.

The greater pluriformity that is possible now in the celebration of the liturgy offers more scope to women to make a creative contribution. One special case that can be mentioned in this context is that of liturgical celebrations in small communities and groups, and the growing practice of house masses. In all these renewals, it is not so much a question of a more equal distribution of functions as of a growth in a "new consciousness" in the Church, in which the equality of men and women becomes a deep conviction. The attempt on the part of women to play their full part in liturgical functions may be blocked by the fact that liturgical life as a whole is passing through a period of crisis. We must hope, however, that women will not be deterred too much by this, because it is only through the interaction of men and women that the liturgy will function in a renewed and meaningful way. It is not so much the interests of women as such that are at stake as the interest of the Church as a whole.

Translated by David Smith

Johanna Klink

Family and Liturgy

THIS is a question which has become increasingly topical in recent years. It would seem as though problems connected with the family are becoming more urgent just as more and more people are ceasing to go regularly to church. Christians without children can be divided very broadly into two camps—those who have gone to church all their lives, regard it as indispensable and are ready to accept changes, and those who no longer find it important to go now that it is not a question of "heaven" or "hell". Generally speaking, the first continue, the second stay away.

This division is not so clear-cut in the case of Christians with families. With their children in mind, these people hesitate between the two poles. Some want to spare their families the experience of church attendance as a duty with which they grew up, yet at the same time want their children to be inspired to faith. Others look consciously for a church where the service or some aspect of it is attractive or interesting to their children. A relatively small number of families are in a position to create their own family liturgy, sometimes at home and perhaps only on special occasions.

Now that the laity are enjoying greater freedom and responsibility in the Church, they are—if they are parents—finding it far more difficult to function as family groups within the Christian community. They are more conscious than people seemed to be in the past that their children are bored at Mass. More and more families find it very difficult to continue to take part with real conviction in the liturgy Sunday after Sunday. Despite the fact that the liturgy is now in the vernacular, that the singing is modern, and that there are many other improvements, parents are at a loss to know how to get their families—especially the older members—to go to church. It seems as though people have broken out of the tight bond that bound them in the past to the liturgy and have thrown it aside for all its improvements. They are apparently unconscious of the freedom that they enjoy compared with the compulsion, the alien language, the solemnity and the "hell fire" sermons that their grandparents knew. Or is it perhaps that the mystical experience of other-worldly holiness that went together with Latin and Gregorian chant is a grave loss that cannot be replaced by the contemporary, deliberately ordinary new liturgy? It cannot be denied that many people no longer go to church because they miss the good old days.

I. Liturgical Community

I had to decline a request by the editor to write on the theme of "family and liturgy" in terms of home services, with or without a priest, because of lack of experience. All the same, the theme has other, equally important aspects, some of which I should like to discuss here.

Parents often make their own liturgies at home with other families because they want above all to escape from the anonymity imposed on them and their children in a large church where detached voices are heard through loudspeakers, and to form a close community in which they are personally involved. They do not want what seems to be a symbolic representation of a meal. They want to share a real meal at which they can actively experience the universal priesthood of all believers. They also often want to go further than the official Church will allow them to go, and to share this meal with other, non-Catholic believers.

This is clearly because people are looking for a deeper meaning in the liturgy, not so much for mysticism or dogma, but for a closer human community of shared faith in which their families can be more actively involved.

II. Only a Part of Humanity

It is only now that we are beginning to realize just how little consideration is given to the family in the Church, which has

always, from the beginning, been a community of men, women
and children, but which has become, in the course of history, a
Church of men and later a Church of unmarried men. Full justice is no longer done to the state of being completely human,
that is, man, woman and child.

The Church is dominated by men. The liturgy, the Councils,
the legal structure, the political power and the pattern of rational
teaching—all testify to this. The Church's authority may even be
the result of the historical influence of the Roman *pater familias*.
The Church is not so much an organism, the body of Christ, as
an institute. Power, authority, legalism, an emphasis on doctrine,
punishment and reward, intimidation—these elements prevail in
the Church and they are all signs of male domination. The man's
attitude is based on authority, the woman thinks in terms of community. Man is naturally a lawyer, woman concerned with personal relationships. Man thinks in the abstract, woman in the
concrete. Why should these male attributes be valid in the
Church and not the woman's? Surely full justice ought to be
done to both in the community of Christ?

The veneration of woman, the "heavenly Mother", that grew
up in the Roman Church would seem at first sight to be a movement away from the male principle, but woman on earth has
none the less continued to occupy a silent, servile position in the
Church. Yet we read in Genesis that "God created man in his
own image, in the image of God he created him; male and
female he created them" (Gen. 1. 27) and we know that Jesus
called mankind to a messianic community.

Throughout its history, the Christian Church has retained at
least one characteristic of the Jewish temple or synagogue, where
men only meet and women are in attendance, without any status
or responsibility, sitting behind bars like spectators watching the
men in action. Women are also in attendance in the Christian
community. Certainly in the liturgy, they are what Paul called
"sojourners" (*paroikoi*; Eph. 2. 19), in contrast to the Christian
"members of the household of God". There is still a tendency in
Christian circles to ignore those passages in Scripture in which
Jesus is shown to have quite a different attitude from that of the
traditional Jews towards women and children. He did not found
another synagogue, but an *ekklesia*, a *qāhāl* or a community of

faith consisting of men, women and children in which the human relationships of the period were reversed.

III. The Messianic Function of the Child

In Matt. 18. 1–6 and Mk. 10. 13–16, we read how Jesus regarded contact with children as a condition for those who wanted to come into contact with God. The person who wanted to enter into a relationship with Jesus and at the same time thrust children aside closed his way to the kingdom of God. Christ himself put a child between himself and his disciples and said, "Whoever receives this child, receives me." If we take Jesus' words to heart, we are bound to recognize that children have a special part to play in the community of Christ. One of the few places where anything explicit is said about Jesus' attitude towards children describes his indignation (Mk. 10. 14) that they should be prevented from coming to him; and another, parallel, passage reinforces this deep indignation by reporting that he would hang a millstone round the neck of anyone who placed a stumbling-block in the way of a child and let him to be drowned in the sea (Matt. 18. 6). These passages have been either by-passed or falsified in the Church, and their true meaning has been missed —the fact that Jesus was addressing adults.

What prompted Jesus to put a child in the midst of those who believed in him as a necessary condition for their coming to him? We can only guess—it may have been the child's originality, small size, insignificance in the adult world and perhaps also his trusting, open nature, all those aspects that affect us. There is still great reluctance in the Church to recognize the child as a full partner in faith, sharing in the responsibility of and with a special function in the community. Resistance to the child in the community of Christ may well be connected with resistance to the Messiah himself, who went straight to the heart of the matter, God himself and his kingdom, and who saw into men's hearts. He was himself, after all, the original Child of God. It may be a very good criterion for whether we are really Christian or not to examine our attitude in the community towards the child and his special function.

IV. STILL NO REAL INTEGRATION

Women and children are, of course, admitted to the liturgy, but it is very questionable whether they have ever been really integrated, in accordance with their essential function, into the activity of the community.

An extreme example of this absence of real integration can be found in the Calvinistic communities, with their emphasis on patriarchal authority and doctrine. In almost all that it does, the Calvinistic community is a community of adults and above all of male adults. The "admission" (!) of women to the office of deacon, elder and preacher has always been accompanied by great resistance, and non-theological factors have always played a large part in this. What are the real reasons why women may not break bread in the community—surely the most obvious task for a woman and mother—and why may they not receive a child into the community by the sign of water, another function that could surely be carried out most appropriately by a woman?

In most Protestant churches, it is an exclusively adult community that shares the Lord's Supper, which children are still not officially permitted to share. Only those who have made a confession of faith—usually at the age of eighteen or so—are "admitted"(!) to the communion table. The Protestant community is typically a community of adults and this is no doubt connected with the traditional emphasis placed on knowledge of the Bible and of Christian doctrine (the Heidelberg Catechism), and on a definitive choice of Christ or an experience of conversion. Children have for a long time been taken to church services, but they have always been "sojourners", not "members of the household of God" and are still to a great extent ignored in preaching and the liturgy.

The pericopes to which I have referred (Matt. 18. 1-6; Mk. 10. 13-16) have also been overlooked or reduced to harmless dimensions in the Protestant churches. Sunday schools are a feature of Protestantism, with the result that there are "para-parishes", "para-liturgies" and whole miniature churches at the child's level in Protestant circles. These Sunday schools are under the direction of established unions, and even now little inspiration is given to them by the "adult" Church, let alone by theologians. The child does not exist as far as the theological faculties are concerned.

In the Calvinistic churches, there is a theological recognition of the child, who is "received into the Covenant" by baptism, but this recognition lasts for ten minutes. The baby is then taken back, by his or her aunt, to the cradle in the consistory chamber and has to wait for another eighteen years before he or she is recognized as a fellow believer and member of the community, after having followed a biblical and catechetical course lasting some fourteen years! In other words, recognition and reception into the community is withheld for one of the most important periods of the young person's life, during which he or she is denied contact with the liturgy and the Lord's Supper.

V. From an Immature to an Adult Community

I have of course given an outline of the Protestant tradition in its most extreme form. There have been many improvements recently—for example, the introduction of special family services in which parents and children can share the Lord's Supper—but on the whole, the Roman Catholic tradition, especially since 1911, seems to have been better in this respect. One has the impression that there is more attention given to children in Roman Catholicism than in Protestantism, but also that this interest has perhaps been more quantitative than qualitative, more directed towards the idea of "increase and multiply" than towards the child as such. The child has perhaps been regarded less as a partner in faith, going before us on the way to the kingdom of God, and more as an object for indoctrination. It is difficult to deny that "para-parishes" have been created in Catholic circles too—the exclusively Catholic schools at which children have been, at least until fairly recently, given a sound liturgical and dogmatic indoctrination, with the aim perhaps of getting them used to the "Catholic way of life" early so that they will stay in it later.

What is the situation, however, with regard to the integration of children into the community of believers? I once went to a "children's mass" in Berne, but nothing in the service indicated that it had anything to do with children. More recently, a "first communion" service gave completely the opposite impression—

the word of welcome was spoken by one child, the confession of sin by another, and the biblical readings were presented and acted out by children after rehearsal at school. The rest of the community was completely passive during the whole service, watching the liturgical play put on by the child actors and readers on the "stage" around the altar. As this audience consisted mainly of adults, it was clear that, here too, the children were seen as a separate category of performers, not as members of the community, fully integrated with the adults.

Is it perhaps true to say that the Christian community has remained immature and childlike despite almost twenty centuries of Christian life? The celebration of the Eucharist itself is a sign of this—hardly a meal, but the administration of a "medicine" to people who open their mouths to receive it. Little children, not adults, are fed in this way. Is it purely by chance that this way of sharing in the eucharistic meal is disappearing just at a time when the Christian community is passing through a crisis of adolescence and is demanding more responsibility?

It may seem contradictory, but I believe that the community will overcome its infantile attitude to the extent that it takes the child seriously as a full member. We have, as Paul said, to attain the *plerōma* as a community of believers, to grow to the fullness of Christ (Eph. 4). We also have to be *able* to grow up in the community and I think that the Catholic Church provides more opportunity for this than the Protestant churches, in its liturgy and in the successive stages of inauguration that are available— baptism followed by first communion, and then by confirmation and the renewal of baptismal vows. In this way, belonging to the Catholic Christian community is not confined to one day, the day on which the confession of faith is made, but consists of a whole process, a gradual inauguration by stages.

On the other hand, although children and young people have more chance of growing to maturity in the Catholic community, the Protestant tradition can be an example to Catholics in so far as it provides the adult with a more definitive initiation for commitment to his Christian task in the world. This, however, implies that there should be a much more fundamental approach to adult catechesis, perhaps from the age of eighteen onwards, especially with godparents in mind.

VI. The Key Position of Parents in the Church

I do not believe that the family has a greater claim to our attention in the Church than, for example, unmarried or old people. A special family mass is too exclusive if it means that the people without families are not to attend it. All the same, it is not wrong to say that parents occupy a very special functional place in the community. Until now, too little consideration has been given not only to the mother and the child and therefore indirectly to the man, but to fathers and mothers as such, the parents who are key figures in the handing on of tradition. It is they who are most intensely concerned, as human beings, with the next generation. So far at least, the school and the Sunday school have tended almost automatically to take over the task of handing on faith to children.

Surely it is rather strange that the Church should call upon parents to have their children baptized, make them promise to bring their children up as Christians, and let them go? Of course, they can send their children to a Catholic school and, although it seems to be very indirect, it is in fact the most direct way of including the parents, making use of them, giving them guidance and inspiration to tell the testimony and the law "to their children, so that they should set their hope in God" (Ps. 78. 6–7).

We shall not integrate the family into the liturgy simply by using folk or beat masses, attractive family services or special school or children's masses. This will at best only serve as a transition towards a more original form of Christian experience in the Church itself.

VII. More than Fellow Humanity

There are many Catholic Christians who would like to return to Latin and Gregorian chant, partly because they would like to find a refuge from the world of noise, violence and war. It may, however, be because they are looking for what is more than ordinary, more than human, for something that transcends the world. But the contemporary prophets have made it clear that transcendence cannot be found beyond the world, but in it.

Partly because of the modern means of communication, however, we have become almost immunized against constant demands, protests, social actions and cries of distress. The theme

of fellow humanity has, even in the Church, become an almost
meaningless refrain. All the same, there is much distress and need
in the world and it would be dangerous to seek a refuge in senti-
mental or aesthetic emotional experiences in the Church. The
Old Testament prophets told us that the liturgy can never be a
service if we do not try to remove injustice from the world.

It is, however, easy to forget that liturgy is more than fellow
humanity and that it has more than a purely social dimension.
One is bound to ask from time to time where all that is going on
now in the Church, especially the attempts to bring everything
up to date, is really leading. Young people can, there is no doubt,
be inspired and encouraged by beat masses and socially or politically slanted services. But where is the element expressed which
may endure beyond this present age and engage the next generation as well? What is really fascinating and of lasting value in
the Church is the transcendent element, the more than human,
totally different factor, without which the liturgy is no more
than human noise or a "clanging cymbal". Parents and young
people will not be held in the long run by pop songs and cups
of coffee after mass. They need to be in contact with the origin
of faith, above all with the original document, the Bible, and
with original symbols of God-with-us and his kingdom in the
world which liberate us, put us in touch with the sacral in the
Church and go to the very centre of our being. They need the
most profound experience of the Church where the whole human
person is addressed at the deepest level.

Anyone who has been seized by this transcendental reality
knows that it is pointless to celebrate the eucharistic meal in
exclusiveness, separated from his brothers and sisters in Christ.
He knows from his own experience that it is "invalid", not according to Jesus' original intention, to celebrate the meal exclusively, even though the words that Jesus first used are repeated
exactly. If "neither death, nor life, nor angels, nor principalities
... nor anything else in all creation, will be able to separate us
from the love of God in Christ Jesus our Lord" (Rom. 8. 38–39),
then no Church and no law governing the liturgy should be able
to do so.

Translated by David Smith

Louis Cyr

The Church Musician

WE ARE at the beginning of a very creative phase in the realm of church music, in which composers, writers and everyone who goes to church services are all directly involved. Those who are officially responsible for arranging services in which everyone is expected to take a creative part are called upon as never before to keep a critical eye on the musical talent available with a view to its possible use in contemporary services.

The church musician, whose training and basic attitude barely equip him to deal with the present situation, may well doubt whether he is equal to the task facing him today. He may therefore seek to excuse himself by talking about the present "crisis" in church music, try to cover up his own impotence by complaining about a general loss of quality, or say that he cannot create music of the kind required now because of loyalty to his office as he has always understood it.

In the present very complex situation, more is expected of the church musician than he is really able to give, and his tasks have become very flexible. We could, of course, follow the traditional method of defining the office of the church musician as precisely as possible and then deduce from this what his office and his tasks should be today. This could be done first by looking back at the past and considering what took place traditionally in the sphere of church music and then reviewing developments since the Council and the official publications that have accompanied these developments. To approach the subject in this deductive way could, however, only result in disappointment—we would almost inevitably end up in a blind alley.

This is because, in any inquiry, three basic questions must be asked—firstly, what kind of music should be used for, secondly, what kind of people; and, thirdly, for what purpose? It is only if these questions are answered in all honesty that the at present untapped musical talents will be able to develop. I shall not attempt, then, to deal systematically with the subject, but simply approach it, on the basis of the experience of most church musicians today, from various points of view. Firstly, I shall look at it from the psychological and physiological point of view and attempt to find out some of the essential characteristics of Church music today. Secondly, I shall consider it from the sociological standpoint, bearing in mind the experience of non-liturgical music which the churchgoer has today and which of course determines his attitude towards church music. Thirdly, I will discuss the specifically theological functions of church music (the theological point of view).

I. What Kind of Music?

Melody and Rhythm in Time and Space

I am not referring here to the usual alternatives—sacred or profane, traditional or modern, serious or popular, and live or recorded music. No kind of music and no technique can be automatically ruled out as unsuitable for worship. Many forms of music-making are, of course, not used in church today because of a lack of diversity in forms of worship, but, in the long run, the only determining factor is the total liturgical structure or that part of it which is to be musical. My aim here, then, is simply to examine some of the essential characteristics of making music in church which—because church music has for so long been so exalted in its style—are often regarded as too lowly and too primitive to be worthy of serious consideration.

Music can, on the one hand, fill a more or less enclosed space with sound and rhythm and, on the other, it can extend in a more or less straight line in time. It takes place, then, in *time* and *space*. It is also accompanied by many other, secondary phenomena. These include, for example, constantly changing volume, short or long, symmetrical or asymmetrical *rhythms*, which may also cause movement and which the human body cannot ignore without harm to itself, consonant or dissonant harmonies produced by one or more voices, long or short and alternately rising and falling *melodic* scales, the pauses that inevitably accompany these sounds, and the at times intoxicating changes of key of which the human ear is often only half aware.

Music can therefore be regarded less as a closed, finished work and more as a dynamic phenomenon which is always becoming, always in the process of coming about. This aspect of movement, spontaneity, discovery, changing emphasis and renewed experience plays a very important part whenever a well-known "work of music" is repeated.

These may be well-known truths, but there are many practical conclusions to be drawn from them, especially with regard to music in the liturgy. The first is connected with the fact that music takes place in time. To reduce it to a legally prescribed minimum as something with which to fill in gaps in the liturgy is therefore to misuse it completely. It is most important not to curtail music at the opening of a church service. People need time to get in tune with each other, to achieve harmony together, to find their voices and to begin to make music well.[1] On the other hand, however, the opening song should not be too long, although experience has shown that short refrains or antiphons are very difficult to sing as integral parts of the whole if they are not firmly enclosed in a very carefully composed, balanced dialogue between the people and the rest of the musical body. All sharp juxtapositions have to be avoided so that the whole rhythmical and melodic pattern can develop smoothly and continuously. All the essential elements in the whole musical body, that is, the organ and other instruments together with the singers (soloist, *schola cantorum*, choir and people), must be able to carry out the role assigned to them, sometimes singing or playing together, sometimes simply listening. Above all, making music in church should not impose excessive demands on the congregation or leave anyone too tired.

[1] See especially Huub Oosterhuis, *Prayers, Poems and Songs* (New York, 1970), especially "The Tent of Meeting", pp. 97–118.

In the second place, all rhythmic and melodic *ostinati* or other elements which may give rise to movement, a feeling of happiness or enthusiasm or even excitement should be encouraged. Surely such effects are completely in accordance with the spirit of worship in the deepest and widest sense?[2] This, of course, confronts us with the urgent need to come to a decision about the type of music that is really wanted in church nowadays. In the nineteenth century, our attitude towards rhythm and the dance (and thus towards such instruments as the double bass and the bass guitar, and towards drum and organ pedal accompaniments) became gradually obscured because of the increasing preference for the style of Palestrina and Gregorian chant. Now, however, we are witnessing a very healthy renewal of interest in rhythm and movement, the result of having taken folk music and jazz seriously for a long time.

The great organ and even the harmonium have many limitations in modern church music. Apart from being obviously unsuitable for accompanying rhythmical singing, they cannot be transported out of the church and used in services with small groups. The piano and the easily transportable instruments of the jazz ensemble or the beat combo are often more practicable in such cases. When, as so often happens, what has already been tried out in the small group is transferred to the large church, there is almost always an explicit desire to use the same instruments, and the great organ cannot always be employed in conjunction with them. Sometimes it has proved better to have a small positive organ, an electronic organ (these organs have been improved so much technically in recent years that it is well worth trying one out on approval) or even a grand piano, all of which can be played alone or with the instrumental group in the church choir.

Thirdly, it is important to remember that these rhythmic, time factors are dependent above all on the spatial relationships, in other words, on the acoustics. It is the space in which the music is sung and played which ultimately determines what instruments are used, how many people take part in the choir, the volume of sound that is produced, and the effectiveness of the

[2] See Harvey Cox, *The Feast of Fools* (Cambridge, Mass., 1969).

pauses. The rhythm and melody of the sound that is made by the community depend on the acoustic space available.

This can, however, be improved by carefully adjusted amplification. The soloist or cantor, the choir and the instrumentalists must, for example, be at the right distance from the microphone and, if the organ or a beat combination is accompanying the singing, the balance must be carefully watched. It is important not to drown weak singing from the congregation, or to try to speed them up by going a few beats ahead of them whenever there is a suitable pause in the music.

There are many factors which contribute to the complete or partial failure of all attempts to make good music in the fullest sense in church. It can so easily be reduced to the rank of an exploited servant, or even killed stone dead—by a soloist or cantor, for example, crushing the people's singing with his own confident, loud tones. The acoustics may be so bad that everyone has the chastening impression that he is singing alone, with the inevitable consequence that he is reduced to silence. One frequent cause of failure is that insufficient time is so often given on Sundays to the service itself, with the result that the organist has no chance of finishing the piece he has been asked to play, the choir has to cut the motet in half, the jazz group cannot improvise, the opening song is curtailed and the very important musical *intermezzi*, during which the congregation can relax, are eliminated. Sometimes, too, there is not enough time for practice in the church before the service. All these factors indicate a failure to take the elements of time, space and rhythm seriously into account; the effect of this on the music is often disastrous.

It should on no account be assumed, because of what I have said above, that I am in favour of doing away entirely with the organist in church. On the contrary—the well-trained and competent organist is more necessary than ever before, but he must now be able and ready to look for and work with all kinds of different instrumentalists, who can supplement his playing and even play without him. He must adapt himself to the new melodic forms and the different ways of accompanying the new songs. Ideally, he ought also to be able to make his own arrangements of such music. He will furthermore only obtain good results from the other instrumentalists and know how to judge their

performance if he knows something about their instruments—
especially the percussion.

Is all this too much to ask of one man? It may well be, in which
case it will be necessary to look for helpers. The choir or schola
on the one hand and the instrumental group on the other ought,
of course, to be led by a choirmaster and a conductor respec-
tively, but these two men, together with the organist, will not
be exclusively responsible for changes in the times and order of
services, the acquisition of instruments, acoustic improvements
and the growth of good music-making in the community. This
will be the responsibility of *all* concerned in the preparation of
services, so that the tasks will be equally shared and as far as
possible everyone may have some say in this question.

Whether or not music is worth so much trouble and thought
will be discussed more fully in the third section of this article.
Here and now, however, before concluding this section, we
should not forget that there is a danger that the music which we
have now, the "traditional" church music, may come to a dead
end and cease to be taken seriously before the new liturgical
music has come fully into use. How, then, is it possible for the
present music to serve as a first stage in the development towards
this new music? This is a crisis with which Protestants have
been familiar for a long time. For four centuries, music has
played an essential part in their services and a great deal of time
and thought has been given to it by organists, choirs, cantors and
the people themselves. Now, however, not for the first time in
their history, they are confronted by the need for change. They
may not have to struggle with the same problems of time and
space that we have, but they are faced with the sociological problem of being embedded in an ossified repertory of neo-baroque
music. This problem, and the theological one, which is also
shared by Protestants, will be considered in the following sections.

II. For what kind of People?

Confronted with the decline in communal singing in church
today, in Catholic circles certainly, many church musicians are
at a loss to know whether the present-day churchgoer still has any
experience of making music with others outside church. This

question is answered in the affirmative or in the negative according to whether the parish concerned is self-contained or whether it is sociologically homogeneous. In addition to this, brave attempts to introduce new music often encounter stubborn resistance from those who favour the "good old days", yet at the same time they also meet with a lukewarm response on the part of those many of the younger members of the Christian community who usually come to church either irregularly or not at all. Permission is reluctantly given for "young people's masses", in which the beat, jazz or rhythmical music that we have been discussing is used, and these may take place separately or else, after having been previously announced, within the framework of an ordinary service. But the real purpose does not remain hidden from the young people for very long—they are a device for winning the young back to the normal services. This inevitably results in a polarization of positions, and at best mutual toleration without any real *rapprochement*. We can hardly speak of communal worship yet (or we can no longer speak of it) and this is regrettable, if it is true that acceptance or rejection of new forms is not always predominantly a question of age or of the so-called generation gap, but rather of attitude.

It is, of course, possible that too much emphasis has been placed on communal singing because we have interpreted the idea of "participation" in too one-sided a way. (In many cases, this led to the abolition of church choirs!) We ought, perhaps to look at the question as to whether people still sing or not on a much broader basis, that of the musical experience or presuppositions that most churchgoers (or potential churchgoers) bring to the liturgy with them. Instead of complaining about the annoyed animosity of those who stay away or the lazy indifference of those who come to services, and instead of going on, in a resigned and routine way, with time-honoured practices, we ought perhaps to do something much more positive. We should take stock of the musical talent that we have at our disposal and build up communal music-making in church services on a more solid basis. We should also ask certain questions. How is music generally experienced nowadays, that is, outside the framework of the church? To what extent can this experience be used in church services? Which tendencies should be avoided and which should be incorporated into worship?

We are not, of course, primarily concerned here with the especially social or sociological function of music in worship, but it is important to note a number of factors which to a very great extent determine music-making in worship and even restrict it considerably.

In the first place, many of those who are concerned with the sociological aspects of music are pessimistic about the deliberate exploitation of music as a consumer commodity and they take a very one-sided and negative view of the debased character of music as pure entertainment. I do not share this gloomy view, but I am convinced of the need to take the consequences of this commercial aspect of music very seriously.[3] In other words, I believe that we have to examine this debased function of music very closely. We must ask a number of questions based on the observed effects of this kind of music. A simple succession of chords and an almost primitive beat—uncomplicated music entirely without surprises—is exploited as a means of giving an illusion of idyllic happiness. This music offers consolation to the lonely, a flight from the dull everyday world and a way of filling in empty time and sometimes meaningless occupations. It also provides a substitute for a frustrated need for movement. Certainly, there is an irresistible tendency for people to allow themselves to be drawn quite passively into this pleasurable state of musical intoxication, becoming physically exhausted when the music reaches its peak of intensity and volume. Our most important questions are these. What is the positive element expressed in this flight from torpidity, this inner vitality? Can part of this element not be integrated into the worship of the Christian community with its task of redeeming the world? At what point does active listening to this music change into a comforting movement away from reality?

In the second place, it must be borne in mind that this is happening now, at a time when revolutionary, politically committed songs of protest are being sung with passionate conviction and

---

[3] T. W. Adorno, *Einleitung in die Musiksoziologie* (Hamburg, 1968); see especially chapter 3, "Funktion", pp. 49–64.

often a deep sense of tragedy by the troubadours of the present generation. The most striking aspect of this phenomenon is that active participation is rare—most prefer to listen quietly and meditatively in the company of others, feeling that this experience speaks directly to them, makes them conscious that a utopia of peace and justice can be created and confirms their conviction that music which does not expose without pity the unjust unchristian powers of their world should not be tolerated. These simple and spontaneous songs are always in danger of moralizing. What is more, these committed singers easily become disillusioned and despairing when they are unable to find an outlet for their suffering in music. Surely their commitment to peace and justice in the world, expressed in primitive or in refined musical forms, can be utilized by Christians in Church services?

Thirdly, radio, television and recordings offer exceptional opportunities for spiritual enrichment, and constantly expanding musical education is enabling more and more people to make music actively or at least to hear music in their free time. These technical aids have made the task of dealing critically with the serious music of the past and the beat and pop music of today easier and this is bound to act as a stimulus to those many musicians engaged in full- or part-time teaching.

A fourth factor that has to be taken into account is fashion in musical taste, which is determined partly by the customer's desire for novelty and partly by the manufacturer's profit motive. The most obvious example of this, of course, is the constant demand on the one hand for the latest classical recordings and on the other for the latest numbers in the hit parade. To keep pace with these changing fashions and with the technical developments outlined in my third point above is much more than a merely superficial quest for "originality". The musician has always to be prepared to add to and improve his repertory, to experiment, to make use of unexpected forms and "works in progress", and above all to trust in the inexhaustible richness of man's creative imagination. He has to have a flexible attitude towards the music of the past, be open to contemporary musical forms and be ready to adapt his ideas to changing situations in music.

It hardly needs to be stressed that church musicians and

composers will also be affected by these factors. They should firstly make use of the latitude available to them between the fixed, annual feasts and the special ceremonies such as baptisms, marriages and funerals on the one hand and services for conferences, pilgrimages or special groups on the other. In addition to this, they must always recognize that well-known carol tunes, for example, can easily become tedious when transferred to another context. The creation of a lasting repertory may have to take second place to the more urgent need to build up certain song formulas which will make a melodically and rhythmically open and flexible communal music-making in church possible on the basis of "memory signals" which are simple enough to begin with but become increasingly complicated and more demanding.[4] The indispensable aids for this are regular rehearsals, adaptable instrumentalists, a good choir and cheap loose-leaf editions of music. Modest and persistent attempts of this kind will lead eventually to a conscious movement towards more stable and artistic forms of music with a deeper spiritual content. These forms will not come about as a result of reforms originating with the central authority.

Fifthly and lastly, now that we have come to the musical scores and the texts of the songs themselves, it is necessary to consider one most important point. How much attention is to be paid to the *text* in communal singing? "How can you sing such out-of-date, pious words? They are meaningless. They belong to the past, to a world of faith that is quite strange to us today." This is something that the churchgoer hears so often now and it is difficult for him to find an answer, especially if he so loves the old melody and is so carried along by the rhythm that he accepts the words without thinking. Another frequent criticism is even more difficult to answer. "How can you turn these new songs, with their doubts about faith, their questioning, their political protest, into music and sing them, instead of doing what their words demand—whispering, groaning and screaming?"

It seems to me that, in using both the older hymns and the new songs in church, we have to bear in mind another factor which lies at a deeper level than the purely intellectual content

[4] B. Huijbers, *Door Podium en zaal tegelijk* (Hilversum, 1969), especially chapter 1, "Liturgische volsmuziek als taal van allen", pp. 9–26.

of the texts—the universal need for ritual or ritualized music.[5] It would be foolish indeed to use the criticisms that are heard as an excuse to perpetuate the singing of good old hymns with their outdated words or to limit one's choice to strictly contemporary, theologically or politically committed songs and texts. Both have a part to play in public worship.

This brings us to the third question which we must try to answer—what is the function of music in church services? Has it any purpose at all? Does making music together in church correspond in any way with the dynamism of Christian worship? Does this happen purely by chance or is there an effective ritual or symbolic contact between the two?

III. For what Purpose?

It is not possible to discuss all the theological and sociological aspects of communal worship here, but a few outstanding characteristics must be mentioned.[6] In the liturgical service, believers are called together to unity in the spirit of Christ. Together they have to proclaim, give thanks for and ask for (*supplicatio*) the victory of life over death, of love over hatred and of peace over war—despite all evidence to the contrary—in a ritual, symbolic act of making the risen Christ present in the community. This calling of Christians together is in itself a sign that they want, for a while, to dissociate themselves from the narrow experience of everyday life, to cease to be self-centred individuals, to open themselves to each other. Physically and in voice and spirit, they come together in a desire to see their individual lives as parts of a total order of salvation that includes all men, to bring together their fragmented, often despairing individual struggles to survive and to reaffirm their acceptance of the hope, reconciliation and love that Christ has made possible. They take part in a service of baptism, for example, to confess their faith, in a service of penance to confess their reconciliation with God and each other and in a funeral service to confess their hope in the future. The

---

[5] B. Huijbers, *Rituelle Musik*, lecture given at the fourth international congress on church music, Universa Laus (Essen, 1971).
[6] H. Rennings, "Zum Gottesdienst Morgen", in H. G. Schmidt, ed., *Zum Gottesdienst Morgen* (Munich, 1969), pp. 5-14.

individual Christian is invited to move forward together with his fellow believers along the path to faith, reconciliation, hope, and so on, in the various services that he attends.

Making music together plays a vital part in this dynamic process, perhaps even an essential part in bringing about the unity of all believers in body, mind, voice and spirit. This music may perhaps not at first appeal to them all. They may find it too primitive or too outdated. But the mere attempt to sing together the same melody and to move together in the same rhythm, expressing as a singing community the same proclamation, thanks, praise and petition, is in itself an act of liberation. It can set the individual free from his purely personal situation as a believer and make him ready to receive the good news that is all too easily inaudible in the noise of everyday life.

Music, then, should not serve to decorate the liturgy or to lull those present into a state of euphoria. It should not be reduced to the prescribed minimum. It should not be regarded as providing a purely aesthetic or exclusively sacred experience. To use it as a tool for the purpose of manipulating the community into a whole is clearly wrong.

On the contrary, the opening song of the celebration of the Eucharist, for example, must be an active ritual sign of the community's desire to join together in worship. The psalm must positively help the people to listen to the proclamation of the word. The singing of the creed and the eucharistic prayer must extend and complete the effects of this proclamation in praise and thanksgiving. Finally, the communion and concluding songs must enable the people to express their hope and sense of reconciliation. It is only if the music is a completely integrated part of the whole dynamic experience of the liturgy that it will be possible to assess the real value of the factors of time, space and rhythm discussed in the first part of this article, and to adjust the balance between singing and listening and between old and new words and music, as discussed in the second section.

We may eventually expect to have liturgical music which is not in any way lacking as music,[7] but which will reveal the full

---

[7] B. Huijbers, *Door Podium en zaal tegelijk*, chapter 4, "Over de artistieke integriteit bij de compositie van liturgische gezangen in de volkstaal", pp. 55–70.

dimensions of man's faith today. All the attempts that are being made to persuade people to *say* together the various antiphons, verses of psalms and parts of the ordinary of the mass, for example, should not make us lose sight of the fact that even the simplest form of liturgy cannot dispense with some kind of communal music-making now. In the long run, the only possible way of participating in an opening antiphon or a psalm is by making it into music. The whole liturgical event does not, of course, have to be a restless succession of words and music from beginning to end, but empty pauses which are not demanded by the verbal and musical pattern of the liturgy itself are equally wrong.

This whole project calls for a very large number of musicians in the widest sense of the word. These people will not be found by increasing the number of official appointments, where these are made, but only by employing voluntary teams, whose task will not be easy, because the situation confronting them is almost without precedent. The first requisite is, of course, openness to new ideas, new texts, new songs and new services on the part of parish clergy, organists, choirs and congregations. This change of attitude may be very slow to take place and educators will have an essential part to play in preparing a new generation in the schools.

It may be that experimentation with this new music could take place at interdiocesan, national and even international level and include not only musicians of all types, but also sociologists specializing in the field of music, theologians and liturgists. This co-operation may eventually go far beyond the frontiers of church music as such and enable Christian worship to develop to an extent unknown for centuries.

Translated by David Smith

PART II
BULLETIN

John Skoglund

Free Churches
(Worship in a Free Assembly)

THE term "free churches" as used in this article refers to those churches which do not have a prescribed liturgy. Some in this group have a recommended liturgy developed by a synodical body, but each congregation remains free to use it, modify it or ignore it. "Free church" is not a denominational designation. It covers a variety of denominations such as Baptists, Congregationalists, Disciples, Menonites, Methodists, Pentecostalists, Presbyterians and other Reformed groups and many smaller Christian bodies. Such variety makes description of free church worship difficult.

Most free churches do not see their worship as lying outside the main stream of liturgical development. They feel that their worship embodies the same essential elements as the so-called "liturgical" churches. They affirm that the liturgical experience is to be found in the celebration of *word* and *table*, and that prayer is man's response to the objective elements present when "the word is truly preached and the sacraments rightly administered". Most free churches would agree with Calvin that the basic liturgical search must go back to the Church of the New Testament period. They see worship taking place primarily when, as in the early Church, a group of believers gather about the Lord's table to sing and pray, to hear the word read and preached, to break bread and drink wine in remembrance of the Lord's death until he comes, and to offer praise and thanksgiving.

While the free churches have much in common in worship with other churches they do have certain distinctive characteristics.

One of these is a striving for simplicity. Those who come from the non-free churches to free church worship feel that it is barren, lacking in colour and almost utterly devoid of ceremony, and in large measure they are correct. Certainly when compared with Orthodox, Roman and Anglican worship, free church worship manifests an extreme simplicity, both in the way in which worship is done as well as the place. The New England meeting houses were built in a rectangular shape and were without ornamentation. Inside, the congregation would sit on straight wooden benches arranged in rows. In the front would be a pulpit and below on the level of the congregation a table. The windows were of clear glass and the wood-work usually painted white. No statues or pictures or stained glass were allowed. Candles were for light and not for ritual. The minister would wear an ordinary suit, or at most a Geneva gown. The service itself would consist of the singing of psalms, prayers, Scripture readings, a sermon or sermons, and periodically the Lord's Supper. All would be done with the least amount of ceremony. While free churches today have moved away from the stark simplicity of their forefathers, there still remains a strong tendency to do all things in the most direct and simple way possible.

Another distinctive of free church worship is congregational responsibility for worship. While the congregation may accept recommendations regarding worship from a synodical or other connectional body it has fundamental responsibility for the ordering and execution of its worship. The congregation will generally designate a responsible body such as the deacons or elders to develop the basic recommendations regarding worship, and assign to the pastor responsibility for the execution of these recommendations.

While the pastor will generally lead the services, lay participation in various parts, such as Scripture reading, prayers, litanies and versicles, is common. In most free churches, if no ordained pastor is available, the congregation may designate a member of the congregation to perform all the functions generally done by an ordained clergyman. In most free churches laymen can preach, administer the sacraments, as well as lead in other ministerial functions.

Active participation of the whole congregation takes place in the singing of hymns, unison and responsive Scripture readings, amens, prayers and litanies, and in some churches simultaneous free prayer and dialogue with the pastor, particularly as he preaches.

Still another characteristic of free church worship is free or extempore prayer. In many free churches the only written or memorized prayer used is the "Our Father". All other prayer is extempore. While such prayer is often created as it is being said, in many instances it has had careful preparation, not in having been written out in advance, but in the formulation of the topics to be covered, and in some measure in a rehearsal of expressions to be used in the prayer. Such is often the case in the so-called pastoral prayer which occupies a central place in much of free church worship and which covers such elements of prayer as confession, petition, intercession and thanksgiving, The pastor thinks through in advance the subjects to be covered in each of these categories. He may even develop an outline, but he relies upon his free expression when he is leading the congregation in the prayer itself.

Even those free churches which rely upon prayer books often depart from the book and substitute extempore or specially composed prayer as the occasion seems to warrant it.

Another facet of free church worship is a free use of the Christian year. In their beginnings these churches rejected most of the festivals associated with the Christian year. Saints days were eliminated, and even the observance of Easter and Christmas as religious holy days was frowned upon by many. Gradually, however, Christmas, Easter and Pentecost have found places of observance in the free churches, and even the more extended periods of Advent, Epiphany, Lent and Pentecost are now celebrated. Free churches do not require lectionary readings and preaching in their services. Their ministers are free to choose their sermon texts and Scripture readings from any part of the Bible. Some churches have published lectionaries as guides, and these are used increasingly.

Another characteristic of free church worship is the infrequent celebration of the Lord's Supper. With the exception of the Disciples of Christ, who hold weekly communion, in most free churches the custom is a quarterly or monthly Lord's Supper, or

even—in the case of a few—an annual observance. This infrequent celebration does not mean that the free churches feel that
the Supper is not important. Rather the opposite is true. When
the free churches began they looked upon the daily observances
of the traditional churches as routine, legalistic, formal and lacking in spiritual vitality. They felt less frequent celebration could
be made more meaningful. They developed services of preparation, and the Supper itself was a special service, apart from the
routine worship of the church. In the case of the Scottish churches
it often covered several days and was held in summer and out
of doors.

The Supper and Baptism are the two sacraments or ordinances
of the free churches. While the preaching of the word is held in
high regard it is not given sacramental status. Foot washing is
practised by some, notably the Church of the Brethren. But this
practice is seen as part of the Lord's Supper, and done as an act
in that service.

Free church worship is undergoing change under the influence
of the ecumenical and liturgical renewal movements. It is not
only looking at its own traditions, but discovering elements of
value in the worship of the traditional churches. The structure
of free church worship as found in most of the current manuals
is in skeletal form as follows:

Preparation:	Adoration
	Confession
The Word:	Reading and Preaching of God's Word
The Table:	Offertory (gifts, elements and self)
	Petition
	Dedication
	Remembrance and Thanksgiving
	Lord's Supper
	Intercession
	Dismissal and Blessing

Hymns, sung psalms, choral anthems, versicles, doxologies and
glorias enrich the service. Contemporary and traditional music
brings the congregation into touch with the musical traditions of

the past as well as the lively musical idiom of the present. Many free churches engage in free liturgical experimentation. Contemporary services often feature rock and folk music as well as multimedia presentations. Possibly, because of their freedom from ecclesiastical control, the free churches can make their greatest contribution to liturgical renewal through creative experimentation in worship.

For a fuller treatment of free church worship see: J. Skoglund, *A Manual of Worship* (Valley Forge, 1968) and *Worship in the Free Churches* (Valley Forge, 1965); S. Winward, *The Reformation of Our Worship* (Richmond, 1965).

William McCready

The Pentecostals: A Social Analysis

THE Pentecostal movement began in the United States in the Spring of 1967, and was centred upon Duquesne University in Pennsylvania. It quickly spread by personal contact to the University of Notre Dame and the University of Michigan State at Ann Arbor. Since its inception there have been many outgrowths, and presently it is estimated that there are about 12,000 persons in about 250 groups. In a 1936 edition of a text on social psychology, Edward Ross states:

> The reaction from a purely emotional religious revival often leaves the cause of real religion worse off than it was at first. This is perhaps why experienced churches like the Roman Catholic have no use for revivals.

Whether there is a use for it or not, there is certainly a Pentecostal movement under way. One reaction that most observers of Pentecostalism in the Catholic Church have in common is: "There is certainly something there." Most of them are also hard-pressed to specify just what the "something" is. Since I am a sociologist and not a theologian I shall ignore the question of the basis in faith for this movement, treat the phenomenon as any other social fact, and attempt to explain it. I have never had any but the most fleeting contact with the Pentecostals—in terms of interviews rather than participation at prayer meetings. Most of my observations will be based on the available literature on the subject.

A useful model for analysing this movement can be found in

the sociological field of collective behaviour. This field concentrates on those occasions of human behaviour when the ordinary normative structures disappear, and co-ordinated behaviour arises and changes under the control of constantly emerging normative definitions. Situations that are commonly treated in this area are crowd reactions, riots, crazes, fads, various kinds of mass social movements, etc. The distinctive mark of all these phenomena is the suspension of the usual controls over impulses and feelings. The person in this situation frequently reports that he felt "free for the first time in his life", or that he felt some terribly heavy burden being lifted from his back. Often one hears that, "I had always wanted to say/do that but I just never felt as though I could". These responses are common collective behavioural phenomena and are frequently reported in the Pentecostal literature. These episodes also tend to occur in settings undergoing some dramatic change or restructuring.

Some of the preconditions that set the stage for episodes of collective behaviour are discussed in the work of Neil Smelser, and are helpful in terms of organizing the field for study. Smelser categorizes collective behaviour into five types: panics, crazes, hostile outbursts, norm-oriented movements, and value-oriented movements. The value-oriented movement is a collective attempt to restore, protect, modify, or create values in the name of a generalized belief. The craze is defined as the mobilization for action based on a positive wish-fulfilment belief. Of these categories craze is the appropriate concept for studying the Pentecostals, since they do not seem to be interested in creating values, but rather in mobilization towards the action of personal conversion.

Four general conditions are necessary if a craze is to appear: (1) a structurally differentiated setting for social action; (2) a relatively well-defined rationality which governs the differentiated setting; (3) a possibility of committing, recommitting and withdrawing resources of flexibility; (4) a medium which can be stored, exchanged and extended to future commitments.

Applying these conditions to the present structure of the Catholic Church in America gives us the foundation for an explanatory model of the rise of Pentecostalism.

The increasing division between the religious and the hierarchical dimensions within the Church has opened up opportunities for choosing options that never before existed. This is to say many people no longer equate authority with religious fervour or excellence. This situation is referred to as differentiated. As an example, we can note the recent movement within the Church to broaden the scope of the individual's conscience with regard to the kinds of moral questions he can answer. People are no longer totally dependent upon a mediating Church to determine ethics and morality. They have differentiated between the "religious" and the "political" dimensions of their Church. The second component, rationality, enters in the sense that there are defined and approved responses for different religious contexts. One response, such as enthusiasm, may be required for the liturgy, while another, perhaps submission to authority, is required for the daily living out of a religious commitment. Control is needed if the various responses are not to be confused. This is supplied by rationality. Increased awareness of the responsibility of the individual conscience has introduced a flexibility into the nature of religious commitment. No longer are commitments eternally binding; instead they can be re-evaluated, and are therefore rendered flexible. Belief in general is seen as a medium which one can spend, accumulate, or lose during the unfolding of one's life in the faith. It fulfils the fourth condition because it can be perceived as something one can have more or less of, and because in a differentiated setting one can vary the intensity of one's belief to fit the immediate situation.

Within the Church itself there is probably no place where these conditions exist more dramatically than in the theology departments of Catholic universities. They are in a prime position to see the increased differentiation as it occurs; to need to evolve a rationality to handle their religious commitments in disparate settings; to experience the struggle of a flexible commitment, both religiously and professionally; and to practise with the medium of belief through the ongoing process of self-evaluation. (Interestingly enough most Pentecostal communities have a theology department somewhere in their background.) Having proposed some conditions which make the appearance of Pentecostalism in the Catholic Church more plausible, let me return to the operating characteristics of this model.

Defining this movement as a craze does not imply that it is a short-term, trivial indulgence of the human spirit's capricious-ness, that might be better termed a "fad". Craze denotes the mobilization of opinion towards the creation of a positive wish-fulfilment belief. This belief usually takes the form of guaran-teeing a positive outcome in an uncertain situation by empower-ing some force, such as the Spirit, with the ability to overcome the ambiguity and anxiety existing in the situation.

In a sense it is the expressed wish that some outside force inter-vene directly in human lives and produce a solution to some diffi-cult problem. People who were very involved in religious struggles on a personal and a professional level felt unable to exert any real influence on the direction in which their Church was moving. A "wish" began to emerge that another answer appear. The Third Person of the Trinity had acquired a reputa-tion over the years for curiosity into human affairs, and thus pro-vided a ready supplier of answers. Several people of like minds and needs happened to meet and a contagious spreading of wish-fulfilment began. It moved through articulate, alienated groups of people at a rapid rate, usually on the medium of personal con-tact. (This begins to display all the signs of classic collective behaviour.) All that was needed now was some bizarre demon-stration of the authenticity of the direct intervention of the Spirit as the problem-solving force.

Perhaps the most publicized and sensational Pentecostal be-haviour is the phenomenon of glossolalia, the speaking of tongues. This has been observed in many Pentecostal settings as well as in other situations including laboratory experiments. Usually it consists of a person or persons speaking and sometimes singing in unintelligible phrases and repetitive sounds. Sometimes an interpretation is offered by other members of the community, sometimes not. If I recall my Scripture correctly, the original Pentecost evoked a speaking of tongues that was the reverse of this present phenomenon. The apostles spoke in their native lan-guages and were readily understood by all who heard them. Now that sort of thing could convince even a cynical sociologist that something out of the ordinary was occurring.

Research into glossolalia has produced some interesting find-ings. Goodman, studying the phonetic components, has deter-mined that the utterances are the artifacts of a trance-state induced as a primary behaviour pattern in the person. Trance is defined as a self-induced delusion. Others have studied the personalities of glossolaliacs and have compiled a list of the traits most commonly found. They appear to be more interested in long-range goals than immediate gratification, they are less realistic and more concerned with feeling than the control groups. They tend to be more humane and tolerant, and in greater need of emotional catharsis, less depressed and less fearful than the control samples. These researchers hold that the speaking of tongues is probably the functional equivalent of a signed contract. It represents the totality of the commitment and provides a ready expression of the same. As a sign of Trinitarian intervention it ranks a bit below tongues of fire and howling winds in its ability to persuade a sceptical scientist, but then perhaps it is not meant for us.

In summary we can say that there is certainly a movement of Pentecostalism within specific areas of the American Church. Using the model of collective behaviour (defined as the "craze") offers some explanations as to the origin and operation of this phenomenon. The Pentecostal movement submits to a natural explanation in terms of a craze responding to religious anxiety and ambiguity. It also contains a technique, glossolalia, for expressing a strong commitment to the positive wish-fulfilment belief. More investigation is required to apply the model more extensively, but this present application seems to introduce some healthy scepticism as to the singularly supernatural origins of the phenomenon.

Herman Schmidt

The Phenomenon of
Spontaneous Groups

I. Spontaneous Groups in the Ancient World

IN THE Hellenistic democracies, the well-being and the development of the people were encouraged by two closely connected factors—from above, the organization of the State, with its officials and its laws, and from below, the legally guaranteed spontaneous and creative activities of the different classes and ranks of free citizens. The nation was protected and at the same time encouraged to expand by families and working groups in the towns and villages. These units provided the means for men to be trained to carry out various tasks in society—in the police and the army, in work such as road, canal and dyke building, in land irrigation, trade, transport, and so on. In addition, festivals and religious ceremonies—including, for example, the striking cult of the dead in ancient Egypt—were organized in this spontaneous way, and financed by men practising the liberal professions and not employed by the State. These services were called *liturgies*.

Originally, these liturgies included social as well as religious services, because no clear distinction was made between the sacred and the profane. Social and religious services were experienced as one and the same precisely because of this spontaneous quality: that is, because they were the free expression of shared humanity and the deepest aspirations of man. With its laws, the State protected this spontaneity in social and religious liturgies, and encouraged their creativity. Whenever the State, fearing disorder and licence, tried to suppress this spontaneity and creativity, conflicts ensued. We may therefore conclude that man has an inalienable right to freedom, which he has to be able to express in a spontaneous, creative and orderly way. Without this, he and society become dead. Not only when spontaneity, creativity and order deteriorate into disorder, licence and arbitrariness, but when they are suppressed by totalitarian rule, man as an individual person and society as a community of persons become repressed and unfree.

In the Septuagint, the term "liturgy" is reserved for services of worship. The conflicts which arose in the Jewish liturgy in connection with freedom of worship are well known. They came about because worship became the province of one of the twelve tribes (the Levites of the tribe of Levi) and because of the rubricization of the liturgy. Again and again, prophets spoke out against this mortal sickness in worship, and in favour of the free, spontaneous and creative expression of the people of God. At the same time, there were of course false prophets who spread disorder and brought the true men of God into disrepute.

The synagogues formed a counterbalance to the strictly controlled official liturgy of Judaism that had arisen in the one temple at Jerusalem. The service in the synagogue usually began with a reading from the Shema and other prayers. A passage was then read from the law and another from the prophets (see Acts 13. 15; Lk. 4. 17), followed by some words of encouragement from one of the members of the community or from a stranger (Acts 13. 15). Jesus and the apostles used this opportunity to preach the Gospel to the Jews assembled in the synagogue (see, for example, Matt. 4. 23; Lk. 4. 44; Acts 13. 5). Finally, the meeting was concluded with the blessing, "The Lord bless you and keep you . . ." from Num. 6. 24–26.

Jesus' prophecy against the Scribes, priests and Pharisees, and his revolutionary action and contestation in the temple, culminating in the tearing in two "from top to bottom" at the time of his crucifixion, can also be seen in this historical context (Matt. 27. 51; Mk. 15. 38; Lk. 23. 45). Jesus after all redeemed man— or "set him free" as we would say nowadays—from the tyranny of ritualism, and gave him the salvation of being able to experience God in spirit and in truth. Through, with and in him a new liturgy came about. With the help of the Holy Spirit, and persevering in faith, hope and love, the Church has continued to celebrate this new liturgy throughout nineteen centuries of conflict and division, on the way towards its ultimate fulfilment in a liturgy of which John has given us a vision in the book of Revelation.[1]

II. Spontaneous Groups and Ecclesiology

At present, Roman Catholic ecclesiology is, of course, dominated by the statements made by Vatican II about the Church, contained in *Gaudium et Spes,* the Decree on Ecumenism, *Unitatis redintegratio,* and above all, *Lumen Gentium.* Attention has, however, often been drawn to a contradiction in the last-mentioned. In Chapter II of this constitution, the Church is defined as the people of God and the universal priesthood of all believers is stressed. In Chapter III, however, apart from a few changes of emphasis (including the idea of collegiality), the whole *Constitutio hierarchica* of the post-Tridentine Church recurs. The inevitable consequence of this contradiction is uncertainty.

Cardinal Suenens referred to this contradiction at the opening of the International Congress of *Concilium* on 12 September 1970:*"It pains us to see that, in Chapter III, it is not sufficiently stressed that the bishops are in* communio *with their local churches.* The words of St Cyprian, 'You must know that the bishop is in the Church and the Church in the bishop', are not sufficiently echoed. The debate—and it was certainly heated enough!—was not primarily concerned with the *collegiality of the churches,* but with the *collegiality of the bishops* as such, quite apart from their vital and permanent union with their priests and people."[2] The consequences of this inner contradiction are well enough known—tensions between the Pope and the bishops, the threat of a *Lex fundamentalis,* the crisis among priests, who, some believe, were "neglected" by the Council, and

[1] The most important studies dealing with the word "liturgy" will be found in H. Schmidt, *Introductio in Liturgiam Occidentalem* (Rome, [3]1966), pp. 33–46. Very many customs which display striking similarities with "liturgies" have been made known to us by scholars of comparative religion and social anthropology.

[2] "De toekomst van de kerk", in the *Report of the International Congress of Concilium at Brussels, 1970* (Amersfoort, 1970), p. 31.

are now placed uncomfortably between the hierarchy and the laity.

Dippel has also drawn attention to another pressing problem connected with the Constitution on the Church and the Modern World: "Anyone who looks soberly and honestly at the situation of the 'Church in the world' and that of the 'world in the Church'... is bound to admit that people have not been prepared ...for a revolution,... and that modern man, including the church-goer, takes it easy with regard to the Church, because he is too busy with other things. A great deal of conformity has crept into the Church in recent centuries and this now constitutes a real danger because of our enormous technical power. The worshipping community is an anonymous conglomerate without real brotherhood. Despite all our work, the 'Church in the world' is continuously losing ground to the 'world in the Church'. A revolution is therefore impossible. For all our preaching and teaching, we are too introverted."[3]

Let us now turn to the Constitution *Sacrosanctum Concilium* on the Liturgy. Two aspects are especially relevant to our problem. In the first place, this constitution gives such a central place to the Church as the people of God that it is in this respect much more consistent than *Lumen Gentium*,[4] with the result that there has been friction at all levels in the Church between those whose ecclesiology is pre-conciliar and those who want to renew the liturgy. A dissonant note is struck in only one article, Art. 22, in which we read that the regulation (*moderatio*) of the liturgy is exclusively in the hands of the *auctoritas* of the Church (the Apostolic See and, *norma iuris*, the bishop), that this *moderatio* is also, by virtue of the "power bestowed by the law" (*potestas a iure concessa*) is also the task of the "competent territorial conferences of bishops" and that no one else, not even a priest, may independently (*proprio marte*) add, take away or change anything in the liturgy.[5]

---

[3] Dippel, *Protestantse verkenningen na Vaticanum II* (The Hague, 1967), p. 229.

[4] H. Schmidt, *Constitutie over de Heilige Liturgie* (Antwerp, 1964), pp. 197–217.

[5] Constitution on the Sacred Liturgy, *Documents of Vatican II*. It would be interesting to see how the words mentioned above in Art. 22 have been translated in the various modern languages.

Until the new Codex is published, there will inevitably be uncertainty about the legal norms concerning the bishops' *moderatio* of the liturgy. The attitude towards the priest reflected in Art. 22 also contradicts that reflected in the rest of the constitution—the fact that he is mentioned here in conjunction with the laity would be excellent were it not for an insinuation that he may be inclined to rebel against the *auctoritas* of the Church. Is the priest, then, not the normal leader of his community in the liturgy? Does he not therefore know, from his own experience, what is best? Yet he is not given the slightest *auctoritas* in the *moderatio* of the liturgy of his own community! Is the priest, by virtue of his *ordinatio*, a servant (*minister*) of Christ and his people (*ecclesia*) under the supervision of his bishop (*episcopus*) and the pastoral guidance of the hierarchy, or is he a servant of the bishop, his immature slave, so to speak? Can his *fidelitas* to Christ and his people not be subjected to great strain if thought of as a slavish obedience to his bishop, to commissions, ceremonies and laws? Surely true collegiality extends as far as the local church, and includes the relationship between the bishop and his priests? Are we concerned here with two "authorities", the bishop placed above his priests, or with one body, the priests under the guidance of their bishop? My final question is this: is the real cause of the crisis in the priesthood not to be found in this absence of clarity with regard to his identity, his office and his position in the Church?

The second aspect of the Constitution on the Liturgy which must be briefly discussed is that the relationship between liturgy and the world is not sufficiently worked out—something which applies to all the documents of Vatican II, except for *Gaudium et Spes*. The liturgy is presented in the Constitution in an introverted way and, even in its renewed form, lacks any real point of contact with the world in which Christians live today and even with the modern Church which is moving towards the world. Nothing is solved by a simple manipulation of the concepts *saeculum* and *sacrum*.[6] In the liturgy, and especially the

[6] For the history of the concepts *saeculum* and *sacrum*, see, for example, H. Fugier, *Recherches sur l'expression du sacré dans la langue latine* (Publication de la faculté des lettres de l'université de Strasbourg, 146) (Paris, 1963); R. Markus, *Saeculum: History and Society in the Theology of St*

aspect of "liturgy and the world", so many unexpected questions have arisen that we can only study the whole problem patiently and critically and in the meantime leave a great deal unanswered.

III. Characteristics of the Spontaneous Groups

On 5 September 1970, the Sacred Congregation of Rites published a third instruction, *Liturgicae Instaurationes*, with directions for the correct application of the Constitution,[7] which provides a good basis for a discussion of some of the questions that constantly arise in connection with the liturgy.

It cannot be denied that, to begin with, Rome and the bishops set an example of freedom, spontaneity and creativity which was followed by priests and Christians in the local churches—with the result, of course, that change brought conflict. Now, however, there is a grave danger that this renewed liturgical life will be stifled by legalism and rubricization. The old routine, the letter that kills the spirit, has returned to the parishes, and passive communities are left uninspired by an outpouring of words. Liturgy is no longer free, spontaneous and creative, but dead.

This is one of the reasons for the exodus from the Church. People no longer find what they had hoped to find in the new liturgy and stay away. They may continue to think of themselves as Christians, but they leave the Church that means nothing to them and does not, in its liturgy, bind them together in a living community. We must blame not the new texts for this, but those who misuse them. Is this very bad situation freely recognized or is it perhaps covered up?—"Of course, there are excesses, but most of our people are still faithful."

There is, however, a positive side to the picture, which is seen in the new liturgy of both large and small spontaneous groups. Partly in order to eliminate misunderstandings about these groups, let me discuss briefly some of their characteristics.[8]

Augustine (Cambridge, 1970); A. Orbán, *Les dénominations du monde chez les premiers auteurs chrétiens* (*Graecitas christianorum primaeva*, 4) (Nijmegen, 1970).

[7] *Acta Apostolicae Sedis* 62 (1970), pp. 692–704; *Archief van de Kerken* 25 (1970), pp. 1089–98.

[8] I am indebted here to F. Haarsma's article "Kleine groepen in de kerken: een nieuw verschijnsel", in *De Tijd* (10 July 1971).

Firstly, these groups do not look at or shrink away from the Church as an impersonal institution. For them, the Church only begins to exist when they experience a powerful sense of togetherness in the *"happening"* of the word and the sacrament, and in its consequences in the activities of their lives. They have made the Church at rest into a Church in action.

Secondly, and closely connected with this, the Church is experienced as a living *communio*, a communion and a community, which is seen as a possible gift and task if it is not automatically present, and as a source of pain and guilt if it is absent. This experience of the *communio* of the Church is, of course, risky, but it is a living experience which can be judged positively by the presence of the "fruits of the Spirit" (love, joy, peace, patience, etc.) and negatively by detachment from the "works of the flesh" (immorality, impurity, licentiousness, idolatry, etc.; see Gal. 5. 19–22).

The third characteristic of these groups is their *charismatic* structure. Every member is encouraged to use his talents to share in the total responsibility of the group. The priest or leader, who is at the service of everyone by virtue of his sacramental charisma and his expert knowledge, stimulates and co-ordinates all the activities of the community by a pouring out of the Spirit during the liturgy. All are involved in proclaiming Christ in the world, not only in word, but in deed.

Fourthly, many of these groups have a *prophetic* and *critical* attitude towards the *status quo* in the Church and society as a whole, which may be expressed either by publicly protesting against or by privately drawing attention to oppression, discrimination or suffering that are otherwise taken for granted. They oppose everything that is contrary to freedom, equality, justice and peace, in the conviction that the Christian community, conscious of the promise of the Kingdom of God, cannot accept such a situation with resignation. They are also especially alert to the injustice and falsehood behind the traditionally fine outward structures of the Church and society.

Fifthly, these groups, with their awareness of the Kingdom of God, are clearly *eschatologically* minded, as the early Christian communities were, living in the expectation of the definitive coming of Christ and his Kingdom (1 Cor. 7. 29–31). Clearly, their aim is to make the original meaning of the word "parish" concrete in the world of today—as "aliens and exiles" in this world and pilgrims on their way to the promised land (1 Pet. 1. 1; 2. 11).

A sixth characteristic is the emphasis that these groups place on *service* to the world, as the counterpart to their critical attitude. We may ask, finally, whether this *political* aspect of the spontaneous groups is not simply an idle gesture, whether it is right to introduce a political note into the liturgy, or whether the way in which political action is taken afterwards is desirable. However this may be, it cannot be disputed that the underlying Christian idea of serving one's fellow men has a place in the liturgy.

The groups characterized thus are doing what was implied at the Second Vatican Council. The word "spontaneity" is the right one to apply to this phenomenon. The other terms used above to characterize these committed groups are highly charged, but reflect accurately enough what is taking place in these communities which attract so many (particularly young) people, and are often known far beyond their territorial frontiers—not merely for their singing. They obviously have something, and this in itself is clear proof that other Christian parishes have little or nothing to offer, and that the spirit of the liturgical renewal has not yet penetrated deeply enough into the life of the Church or has somehow been prevented from doing so.

It would, of course, be wrong to say, purely subjectively, that everything that does not appeal to *me* is not liturgy. There are, after all, people of all shades of opinion in the Church. Paul VI shocked a number of respectable citizens when he welcomed hippies on 16 April 1971;[9] and later, in his address at the eighth conference of the Italian bishops on 19 June,[10] he expressed a genuine interest in and sympathy for spontaneous groups.

Life is not easy for these groups. Generally speaking, they receive little support and are subject to attacks from conservative Christians, who do not hesitate to use press campaigns and even violence to counter them. They are often feared, viewed with

---

[9] *L'Osservatore Romano*, 17 April 1971.
[10] *L'Osservatore Romano*, 20 June 1971.

suspicion and accused of sectarianism, which of course tends to drive them into isolation and to make them become precisely what they wanted to avoid becoming—schismatic sects. Man cannot live and grow, alone or in community, without taking a risk. The members of these groups are not all saints, but this is all the more reason for a Church which calls herself a "Church of sinners" not to turn away from them, despite their apparent waywardness. They are the Church's own children and they manifest above all the promise of new and unsuspected possibilities. As has happened so often in the Church's history, there are seeds here of a painful misunderstanding—the children are in danger of denying the mother Church's traditional heritage, which is in fact really sustaining them, while the mother Church fails to recognize her own deepest inspiration in what they are doing. All the same, resistance to these groups in the Church may have a purifying effect. Throughout the history of the Church, so many of the most promising initiatives taken at the grass roots have encountered obstacles in the institutional Church. The frequent defamation and even persecution of new organizations and religious orders within the Church has often resulted in their being purified before they have come to be fully accepted as positively valuable.

IV. The Creativity of Spontaneous Groups

These groups are quite remarkably creative—during the past ten years, thousands of original prayers and liturgies have been published as well as countless records and tapes.[11] Most of this contemporary source material has still to be studied. Far too

---

[11] See H. Schmidt, *Bidden onderweg van 1960 tot 1970* (Haarlem, 1971). This is a first attempt to evaluate the creative writing of prayers during the past ten years. I have discussed 642 publications and included two hundred quotations as illustrations. After my book was published, at least another six hundred publications have appeared. I have been able to build up a small library (a total of some ten yards of books) and a discothèque of contemporary religious music (consisting of three hundred records). I cannot even name the most important titles, partly because this would be a subjective judgment which is always changing, and partly because I would have to select what is especially valuable from each book. What is particularly striking is the great interest in the Bible and the liturgy as such.

often, adverse judgment is passed on it before it has been seriously considered, simply on the basis of a chance experience of it, of hearsay, or of a short report in a newspaper.

It is hardly surprising that there is a great deal of chaff among the wheat—this is also the case with the older sacramentaries and hymn books. Even if only ten per cent of this material is of lasting value, then we have the beginning of a set of new liturgical books with texts and music drawn not only from the past, but from the present. Anyone who, like myself, knows what is being done creatively today must find it impossible to sweep everything aside in an all-embracing excommunication. We must not make an idol of the new official normative mass in our antipathy to everything—good crops and weeds—that grows spontaneously from the soil.

The Commission for the Implementation of the Constitution on the Sacred Liturgy sent an instruction on 25 January 1969 to the presidents of the bishops' conferences and the liturgical committees containing several norms for the translation of the Latin texts. In the last number (No. 43), a statement was made which is relevant to our theme: "For a completely renewed liturgy, we cannot remain content with texts translated from other languages. New creation will be necessary. None the less, the translation of texts from the Church's tradition continues to be an excellent discipline and a necessary school for the editing of new texts, so that the 'new forms grow as it were organically from the existing forms' (*Constitution on the Liturgy*, Art. 23)."[12]

V. The Pluriformity of Spontaneous Groups

One of the most striking aspects of this phenomenon is that there are so many different kinds of spontaneous groups. Firstly there are the living parishes, in which groups of people first experiment alone with the liturgy and then share their experiences in the parish with others. Groups which shut themselves off from others in the celebration of their own liturgy not only fail to serve others, but become introverted, and ultimately wither away and die.

[12] *Notitiae* 5 (1969), p. 12.

Other groups, the value of whose contribution is not always sufficiently acknowledged, are engaged especially in celebrations of baptism, first communion, penance, marriage, the anointing of the sick, funerals and the word of God.

There are also social groups whose work also has a liturgical aspect. These groups encourage the formation of youth clubs and spontaneously look after old people and the sick. Politically committed groups also frequently like to place their activities within a liturgical setting and to confront the political questions of the present with the reality of the Bible.

All these and other groups are dealing with a typical modern need—to change the anonymous conglomerate into a brotherhood of men—and it is therefore not surprising that liturgy is necessary for them. It is also necessary for them, in their search for their identity and for the meaning of Christianity and the liturgy in their own special circumstances, to experiment liturgically. Sometimes their experiments are irresponsible, but we must try to understand this, even if we cannot explain it. If we tear these experiments out of their context, we tend to be outraged by them and see mere imperfections as serious threats to the very existence of the liturgy, with resulting conflict and discord, at a time when so many basic problems are being debated.[13] Many of these experiments are also more traditional than they seem at first sight to be.

Although understandable, it is still a pity that the original plan of a "normative mass" could not have been realized and that a *Missa sine populo* could find its way into the new missal (how is this possible?), but so little attention be given to the special circumstances of these groups. There is an instruction (*Actio Pastoralis*), dated 15 May 1969, dealing with masses for special groups but this is written as though its authors were unaware of the developments of the last three years.[14]

There is also one kind of group which deserves our greatest

---

[13] In my collection (see above, note 11), I have many loose-leaf books and folders containing not only the texts of many different groups, but also detailed explanations of the techniques used in celebration and a discussion of the problems involved. The publications are intended as instructions for group leaders and as material for study. They constitute a new kind of liturgical publication and call for the attention of liturgists.

[14] *Acta Apostolicae Sedis* 61 (1969), pp. 806–11.

care and sympathy in a true "Church of the poor". The experts who are familiar with the situation in homes for deaf, blind and dumb people, handicapped, mentally sick and retarded adults and children, for the aged and infirm and for deprived young people, tell us that an ordinary liturgical celebration is usually out of the question in such establishments. It should be possible to create special liturgies, with the help of modern technical means, for deaf, blind and dumb people as well as for others in special circumstances. Although it should not be so, the *Missa cum populo* is usually celebrated in such places. Surely the people are not there for the sake of the missal—the missal should be there for the people.

I have spoken of extreme cases of need. But surely the same applies to groups of people whose situation is less extreme, but who none the less suffer, are in need and deserve our attention in a "Church of the poor"? Can those priests and their lay helpers, who gather together in brotherhood groups of people from, for example, the poorest districts, the world of the homeless and the outcasts, or the underworld of sex and drugs, celebrate the Eucharist from the new missal? They cannot. What they need is not the best that professional liturgists can produce, but something totally spontaneous. They must be, and very often are, able to proclaim the love and forgiveness of God, to celebrate a Eucharist in praise and thanksgiving for the merest sign of *metanoia* on the part of these inhabitants of the dark area of society, to make the community of love in Christ present in so convincing a way that it can really be said, "See how these Christians love one another". This spontaneous liturgy may be technically faulty, but it comes from the heart and, under the circumstances, nothing else is possible. When they succeed, these groups of priests and lay people have an experience of Christianity that others may well envy. They are perhaps saints of a new kind and the Church, as in the past, does not know how to deal with them.

My conclusion is positive and certainly not too severe. These priests and the collaborators—unordained deacons and deaconesses—live in the world and are concerned with every possible kind of activity, care, misery and difficulty. They are absorbed in the spontaneous and creative task of christianizing the world, so that celebrating the liturgy is never a routine, but something that demands constant tension and dedication and results in happiness. They know that they often fail, that they make mistakes and that they need help. But if they are frustrated in this task, their situation in their communities at once becomes impossible and they have eventually to leave. This brings us face to face with the problem of the crisis of the priesthood, a crisis so often expressed in question form—"How is it that so often the best priests are the ones who leave?"

The phenomenon of spontaneous groups that come about and disappear is one that has to be taken very seriously. It is often said, especially by conservative Christians, that they last no more than five or ten years. If this is true, then we must try to answer the question, "Why do they last no longer than this?" Those most involved in this movement—their attitude may be positive, negative or simply doubtful—are priests and their closest lay collaborators. Everyone is agreed that there must be some legislation, but no one can say with certainty what form these measures should take.

I admit without hesitation that many groups are guilty of foolish behaviour and can hardly be called Christian. Their activities are often reported in the press and this gives all spontaneous groups a bad name. But how often I have heard others in the present liturgical movement express what I myself have experienced: "What an unforgettable liturgy that group had—what a pity it is forbidden!"

Translated by David Smith

PART III
DOCUMENTATION
CONCILIUM

Brian Newns

English Liturgical Legislation
since the Council

IN England there has been little liturgical legislation in the strict
sense since the Council, though guidance has been given to priests
on the implementation of liturgical reforms as they have appeared. The regulation of the liturgy has to a great extent been
left to individual bishops, but attempts have been made to preserve a certain uniformity of practice throughout the country.

English was introduced into the mass on the first Sunday of
Advent 1964, and the English and Welsh bishops sent a joint
Instruction to their clergy on the new form of Mass and the introduction of the vernacular. Practical suggestions on the celebration of mass were also issued. Both of these documents
envisaged the use of lay readers.

The hierarchy itself has issued no instructions about concelebration but individual bishops have given general permission for
it in their own dioceses. General permission was given for communion under both kinds for all cases mentioned in *Eucharisti-
cum Mysterium*, n. 32, to take effect from 15 August 1967. In
1971 the hierarchy decided, as a result of the Roman instruction
Sacramentali Communione, that individual bishops should de-
cide for their own dioceses when communion might be received
under both kinds, but that it should not be granted to children
of primary school age.

With the appearance of the new *Ordo Missae*, introduced on
the first Sunday of Lent 1970, the bishops decided that there
should normally be three readings at mass on Sundays and holydays of obligation. In accordance with the *Institutio Generalis*

133

Missalis Romani permission was given for women to read at mass; this concession is to be used sparingly and men readers are to be trained wherever possible. The kiss of peace was initially restricted to small groups as an experiment but in 1971 it was extended to any parish wishing to introduce it.

Communion is normally received kneeling but the practice of receiving communion standing seems to be growing and is permitted. On the other hand the bishops have not as yet sought permission for communion in the hand nor for the distribution of communion by approved laity.

In a statement to the Latin Mass Society in 1968 the hierarchy said that masses in which the ordinary is said or sung in Latin must be retained. Individual bishops have generally insisted that one mass a week should be a Latin mass, and some have required this weekly Latin mass to be on Sunday.

In November 1966 the National Commission for Catholic Church Music issued a statement authorized by the hierarchy, permitting the singing in English or Welsh of those parts of the mass hitherto sung in Latin. It also permitted the singing of suitable hymns or metrical psalms at the introit, offertory and communion, encouraged the formation of choirs and insisted on the preservation of the Latin sung mass. In 1969 the same commission produced a longer document, *Music in the Mass*, in which the same topics are discussed and which permitted the use of other musical instruments besides the organ in church, provided the local bishop approved. In this same year the hierarchy approved the use of tape-recorded music in church, at the discretion of the local bishop, provided it was used to accompany singing and not as a substitute for it.

There has as yet been no national legislation on group masses and house masses, but they are not uncommon in some dioceses. Several bishops have given general directives for such masses, allowing them for various reasons.

The hierarchy has made no rules for the baptism of infants and the preparation of the parents, but J. D. Crichton's booklet *Companion to the New Order of Baptism* has the status of a quasi-official directive. In this booklet the importance of the preparation of parents is stressed. Where they have insufficient faith to make the promises required Fr Crichton counsels that baptism should be delayed but not refused, for the request for baptism is itself to be seen as a positive sign.

Following upon the publication of the *Enquiry into Baptismal Practice*, undertaken by the British Council of Churches with Catholic participation, the hierarchy has directed that the baptism of the principal non-Catholic churches in England be recognized as valid. The hierarchy has also produced a *Directory concerning Mixed Marriages*, a commentary on the papal *Motu Proprio* of 1970 on mixed marriages. The bishops' *Directory* gives general permission for the celebration of mixed marriages within a mass, provided the non-Catholic partner has been baptized. The English marriage rite itself includes the civil requirements for the solemnization of marriage, namely the legal declaration of freedom and the opening words of the formula of consent.

There has been no legislation concerning the sacrament of penance, though some have followed the example of the Scots bishop of Galloway, who in 1968 introduced into his diocese the practice of children making their first confession about the age of nine, after their first communion. Penance services are relatively uncommon, and when held do not include sacramental absolution.

Lastly, it is worth mentioning the *Pastoral Directory for Church Building*, the directives of the hierarchy to all concerned in the building of churches. This was produced by the National Liturgical Commission of England and Wales in 1968.

Philippe Rouillard

Liturgical Legislation in France

THE term "legislation" is wide-ranging since it is the community which legislates; nevertheless, for the purposes of the present survey, I shall restrict myself to the main decrees and directives of the French hierarchy. It seemed of little value to take this account back beyond 1966 or 1967, and it had to stop at 15 September 1971. I shall examine in turn the legislation relating to the mass, to infant baptism, to penance, to the anointing of the sick, and to funerals.

From 5 February 1968, women have been able to act as readers at mass (except for the gospel) and to lead the assembly in singing (*Doc. Cath.*, 1968, pp. 437–8). Of course the use of male lay readers is an established practice, and poses no problem.

More important measures have been taken in regard to the distribution of communion. Communion in the hand is authorized in France (or—more precisely—in all the dioceses where this decision has been taken) since 29 June 1969. This method of taking communion is not to be made obligatory and its introduction should be accompanied by the necessary catechesis (DC, 1969, pp. 672–4).

Communion under both kinds has also been authorized in France since 29 November 1970, but each bishop retains the right to permit or refuse this measure in his own diocese and to lay down the conditions (DC, 1970, pp. 1026–7). The bishops of the Northern Province, for example, decreed on 24 December 1970 that communion in both kinds should be given at Sunday and holyday masses as soon as the faithful were spiritually ready for it (*Eglise d'Arras*, 8 January 1971).

Distribution of communion by laymen is a practice that has spread to several dioceses since February 1969 (DC, 1969, pp. 346–7). On 5 May 1970, the episcopal liturgical commission extended this possibility to the whole of France: as far as each bishop might think it opportune, men and women (but not children), lay or religious, could give communion in or outside the mass, and take it to the sick (DC, 1970, pp. 311–17).

In addition, the celebration of the Sunday mass on the Saturday evening has been authorized since 15 January 1969, as the result of a request made to Rome by the president of the French bishops' conference (DC, 1969, pp. 116–19).

Masses for the young were the subject of a memorandum of the episcopal commissions for liturgy, youth and religious education published in July 1968. Without offering any legislation in the strict sense, this document drew the attention of responsible parties to the legitimate requests of young people in regard to masses organized by and for them: a connection between life and liturgy; a true welcome for the word of God, participation in the homily, and universal prayer; the use of songs and music which would allow them self-expression (DC, 1968, pp. 1419–23). Since then, the hierarchy has not returned to this question, which should first of all develop of itself. On the other hand, in February 1970, the episcopal liturgical commission published a memorandum on small-group masses which adapted to the French pastoral situation a Roman instruction on the same subject. The principles laid down in this memorandum are certainly judicious, but its practical directives seem too detailed to allow of application to the various situations and to the atmosphere of spontaneity characteristic of group masses in general and domestic eucharists in particular (DC, 1970, pp. 278–83).

In the matter of infant baptism, the French episcopate has tried for some years to introduce a certain delay between the request for baptism and the actual ceremony, which would permit of a real preparation of the parents. A document approved by the plenary assembly of the episcopate on 6 December 1965 even then recommended that "there should be a certain delay between the registration of the child, which might well come before its birth, and the celebration of baptism" (DC, 1966, pp. 458–65).

This recommendation took effect gradually, as public opinion became used to it. From March 1966, the bishops of the Paris area decided that the request for baptism should be entered in a parish register and that baptism should be administered only some weeks later when the parents, aided by the priest, had considered the religious implications of the step they were taking (*Semaine religieuse de Paris*, 5 March 1966). The other French bishops took similar decisions between 1966 and 1970. One interesting project for infant baptism in stages introduced in Marseilles in March 1970 is worthy of note: the registration of the child is the first liturgical stage in the celebration of the sacrament; baptism itself can then be administered on a short- or long-term basis (*L'Eglise d'aujourd'hui à Marseille*, 29 March 1970).

Communal celebrations of the sacrament of penance were encouraged by the episcopal liturgical commission in a memorandum of 25 February 1967, which nevertheless insisted that confession and absolution should remain private and secret (DC, 1967, pp. 665–6). Efforts continue to be made in this area, but no other measure has been taken to date.

While awaiting publication of the new ritual for the anointing of the sick, the episcopal liturgical commission published (in September 1970) a text on the communal celebration of the anointing, authorizing the use of the ritual employed at Lourdes for such celebrations since the summer of 1969 (DC, 1961, pp. 235–7). The commission also published (in 1971) a provisional ritual for the individual celebration of this sacrament.

In regard to the burial of the dead, a decree of the Bishop of Autun of 12 March 1971 decided that "there would be a favourable reception for any request for church burial for any one who gave evidence of his attachment to the Church, whatever his situation in canon law" (DC, 1971, pp. 391–2). This measure, which was in line with the practice of a number of dioceses, applied particularly in the case of the divorced and remarried, who were excluded from the sacraments.

In these various areas, the French bishops have been faced with the dual task of putting into practice (with the requisite modifications) the decisions taken in Rome with regard to the whole world, and in which they had often collaborated, and of answering the actual needs of the French pastoral situation. They have acted without haste, in the belief that legislation derives from life and does not precede it.

Translated by John Griffiths

Franz Nikolasch

Liturgical Legislation in German-speaking Countries

IN THE last few years, the Roman reform of the liturgy has been realized in many areas, and as a rule has allowed the individual hierarchical conferences the possibility of adaptation to local traditions (at least within certain limits). In some cases the Roman principles were to be treated as a model. This has made it necessary for the bishops' conferences to lay down principles of action for their particular areas, but in conformity with the basic requirements.

The space allowed me makes it possible only to summarize the most important decisions of the German-speaking bishops' conferences. As a rule Germany, Luxembourg, Austria and Switzerland, because of meetings and contacts between the various liturgical commissions, were able to arrive at common decisions, even though not in all cases simultaneously.

The celebration of the mass is by far the most important area of concern in the decisions of the bishops' conferences. After the publication of the Roman *ordo*, the issue of a provisional German translation for facultative use from the first Sunday in Advent 1969 was agreed upon in Autumn 1969. The basic consideration here was that the Roman missal had not yet appeared, and that only when it did appear, i.e., from Advent 1970, would the new *ordo* be universally binding. There was therefore a possibility of introducing the new form in stages, and thus avoiding any excessive demand on parishes.

The provisional German *ordo* features a number of differences from the Roman version which depend either on already existing liturgical legislation or on article six of the general introduction. The changes consist of an extension of the options for the texts of the invitation to confession (which may be freely expressed), the request for forgiveness, the invitation to the Our Father, and the confession of faith (in which case the Nicene creed may be replaced by the Apostles' creed or a credal hymn).

In addition, the responses after the readings were open to re-formulation or could be retained in their previous form; consequently the versicles are not given in the German edition. In the texts accompanying the offertory the people's responses are also absent. The text itself is usually spoken softly by the priest. If there is no singing, or, if the organ is played, it can (but ought not to) be said aloud The *"Orate fratres"* is said by the priest alone as an invitation to the offertory prayer, and not alternately with the people. A more important change was made in the case of the rite of peace: the prayer was divided into an introduction and a special prayer; the formulation of the invitation to the kiss of peace was left open, as was the kiss of peace itself. The quotation from Revelation was made optional and placed after the quotation from Matthew (8. 8).

In regard to the choice of alternate hymns, the existing special permission for German-speaking countries was preserved: for the entrance rite, additional kyries or the organ are permitted; corresponding rules apply to the offertory and communion. Instead of the responsory psalm, other psalms or corresponding hymns are permitted.

An important decision was taken regarding the new pericope order, which until now has been made binding only for Sundays and holydays. For those days and occasions on which the Roman *ordo* provides three readings, only one of the first two readings is absolutely necessary: this usually means choosing the one that fits the gospel.

These are the most important decisions regarding the liturgy of the parish mass. For special celebrations and groups, individual guide-lines have been issued in the meantime, which try to accord more appropriately with specific situations. Hence some directions for small-group masses were issued which apply to groups established out of common interests, who find that in a small circle they can experience the community character of the

Eucharist better than in the parish service. Examples of such groups are family and neighbourhood, youth and school assemblies, but also marriage and memorial, jubilee or sick-bed services. The guide-lines agreed in Autumn 1970 by the German, and in Summer 1971 by the Austrian bishops' conferences, try to preserve all the essential elements of the eucharistic celebration and yet to answer present demands more proficiently than the corresponding Roman instruction of 15 May 1969. In addition to simplifications of the rite, it is laid down in regard to the priest's vestments that "in exceptional cases the same basic distinguishing vestment allowed for the administration of all other sacraments should be permissible, though of course the stole should never be dispensed with". In regard to the homily, the statement of actual reasons for thanksgiving, and the formulation of addresses, the guide-lines accord with the French instructions.

A special division consists of children's services. Even in September 1969, the German bishops' conference confirmed that "in accordance with article six of the general introduction, the long-practised custom of celebrating the liturgy of the word with children in a form concordant with the faculties of children (while preserving the basic structure of the liturgy) should be preserved". Proposals to this end were formulated subsequently and sanctioned by the bishops' conferences. The following are replaceable elements of the entrance rite which are open to free reconstruction: entrance procession, entry address, children's greeting of one another, tape-recordings or gramophone records and pictorial meditations. Contemplation of a picture and mime are mentioned among the forms of response to readings. These guide-lines were confirmed in mid-1970 in Germany, and as a three-year experiment in Switzerland. In Austria they were approved in Spring 1971 for a one-year experimental period and restricted to a few parishes; special emphasis was laid on the avoidance of too intensive catechizing and on the active participation of the children in the celebration. Work is in progress on an order for the second part of the mass.

There is a special form for masses with deaf children, in which case a particularly intensive simplification of the texts was necessary. The corresponding mass book is to appear in three sections, the last containing the full people's text, the middle section simplified and adapted texts, and the first section the very initial texts. These texts were reproduced in *Gottesdienst* for 7 October 1970.

One of the most important of the detailed regulations concerning the celebration of the mass is permission for lay preaching. In Summer 1970, the Bishop of Graz (Austria) allowed the laity to preach, even though he restricted this permission to a specific time and parish; the agreement of the parish in question was necessary. Among conditions required by the bishop were credibility arising from the witness of a Christian life, and evidence of corresponding training (a completed course of study, a correspondence course in theology).

Already in Autumn 1969, the Swiss bishops' conference had permitted lay preaching "in principle and *ad experimentum*" for a period of three years; the conference laid down no specific rules but mentioned the need for a reference from the theological commission and recommended further study of the whole complex of associated problems during the experiment.

In Autumn 1970, the German bishops' conference issued guidelines for lay preaching which were also published in Austria in Summer 1971. In the individual case, permission is to be granted through the priest responsible and on the bishop's behalf: any long-term commission is reserved to the bishop. Prerequisites for permission are adequate theological formation and homilectic ability as well as special acquaintance with the matter in question or the particular audience.

Since 1969, the entire German-speaking area has enjoyed permission for the administration of communion by the laity. Permission can also be given to women, and can be extended to the communion of the sick. The sole prerequisite is the existence of pastoral difficulties for the priest or deacon. It is stressed that the lay person's clothing should be appropriate to the service.

In regard to the question of communion in the hand, Cardinal Döpfner had already applied to Rome on behalf of the German bishops' conference, and on 6 July received a reply from the Congregation of Rites which stated that the German bishops could allow communion in this way. However, this permission was immediately withdrawn since the Pope had ordained that the whole episcopate of the Latin Church should first be consulted on the problem. In Summer 1969, first in Germany, then later in Switzerland and in Austria, the bishops were able to permit the faithful to receive communion either in the hand or in the mouth. Practice shows that both forms can be used simultaneously without any concrete difficulties.

With regard to communion in both kinds, the bishops' conferences released in Spring 1971 directions on the Roman instruction of 26 June 1970. A remarkable feature of these guide-lines is that they are not governed by the kind of thinking that delights in casuitic rules. In general, no celebration of mass is without the possibility of communion in both kinds: actual practice depends on pastoral criteria and practicability. General permission is given for all cases named in the Roman instruction; in addition, for all smaller communities and for feast-days when the number of participants is not too great. Use may be made of the permission both for an ordinary Sunday mass as for a major feast.

The use of rhythmic chants was for a long time a problem in the celebration of the mass. In Spring 1966, the German bishops' conference declared: "So long as the liturgical appropriateness of any music with jazz- or jazz-like elements is still unclear, experiments of this kind are not permitted for eucharistic celebrations. Experiments on other occasions are subject to the discretion of the diocesan bishop." The other German-speaking countries did not issue such decisive pronouncements but showed greater tolerance. In 1969 the Federal German conference of youth chaplains asked the bishops' conference to "reconsider the decision of Spring 1966". The answer contained a modification which was in any case anticipated by reality: "The decision of 1966 regarding the use of rhythmic songs in eucharistic celebrations is modified to the extent that professional musicians are requested to carry out controlled experiments in order to help reach an answer to the still open question of the liturgical appropriateness of this kind of music. In all circumstances, care is to be taken that the text should accord with the dignity of the eucharistic celebration and the function of its individual parts. Controlled experiments are to be understood in the sense that the use of this music in eucharistic celebrations is permitted in agreement with the responsible musical commissions." Since a general prohibition had been issued neither in Switzerland nor in Austria, the bishops' conferences of these countries were able to avoid a re-tractation of this kind.

The regulation recognizing services of the word with distribution of communion as fully valid Sunday services also seems important. In the resolution of the "Divine service and the Parish" working committee of the Trier Katholikentag of 1970 we read: "On occasion, on the pattern of the practice of the Eastern churches, participation in the Sunday celebration of the Eucharist should be replaceable by participation in a non-eucharistic service." Accordingly, the Limburg official diocesan news-sheet No. 120 of 1970 includes among regulations for week-ends and holidays: "In cases of necessity, the services on Sundays and holidays can be so arranged that there is only one celebration of the Eucharist and additional services of the word with distribution of communion conducted by assistants. . . . The Sunday duty is fulfilled by attendance at such non-clerical services."

The foregoing is a summary account of the more important decisions in the area of the Eucharist. It should also be remarked that a mass of the previous night, i.e., the fulfilment of Sunday duty by attendance at the Eucharist on Saturday evening, has been introduced almost universally after some initial delays, even though here—as in many other areas—the legal regulations have lagged behind actuality.

Of great importance after the renewed celebration of mass is the rite of infant baptism, which was decided upon in Spring 1971 by the bishops' conferences. It is by and large a matter of the Roman model rite adapted at certain points. Already in 1970, with the publication of a provisional study edition, the Austrian bishops' conference had decided among other things that the use of catechumens' oil should be made optional but that the post-baptismal anointing should remain. The bishops' conference also pleaded for retention of the epheta rite and for the addition of the doxology to the Our Father. The final edition contains detailed indications for a discussion with parents before baptism. The prohibition of house baptisms was softened, in so far as any danger to the child's health or any too great distance from the church was recognized as a valid ground for the practice. In the rite itself signing with the cross was shifted to after the homily.

One burning problem (as everywhere) is the question of the

sacrament of penance, above all the problem of whether a communal service of penance without any individual confession can effect an absolution of sins. At the Trier Katholikentag of 1970 the resolutions contained the following remark: "The question whether services of penance are of a sacramental nature should be resolved." Similar requests had already been made at diocesan synods. In an instruction for services of penance the general vicariate of Trier remarks: "Since the essential elements of penance are contained in the penitential celebration, it contains a genuine remission of sins" (*Kirchl. Amtsblatt*, No. 34, 1970). On the same problem, the pastoral letter of the Swiss bishops' conference on penance and confession states (1970): "It is theologically possible that the Church will change its present practice.... The bishops are prepared to persuade the highest levels in the Church to resolve as soon as possible the question of the possibility of sacramental absolution after a general acknowledgment of sins."

As far as marriage services are concerned, work is still in progress: in 1969 the Institutum Liturgicum of Salzburg produced a study edition of the Roman model rite which was introduced facultatively by the Austrian bishops' conference and some German dioceses, in which, however, deviant elements of the German marriage service (*Collectio Rituum*, 1950) could be retained. The goal of renewal will be to respect the Roman model while preserving valuable local elements and taking the present understanding of church marriage into account. Special attention is to be paid to the marriage of partners of different confessions by ministers of both confessions. In Germany the bishops' conference and the corresponding Evangelical body have adopted a dual ritual which enables both ministers to contribute to the service according to the understanding of marriage current in their respective churches. In Austria a similar proposal for the cooperation of non-Catholic ministers has been put forward, but has not as yet been finally agreed upon.

The renewal of the burial service will be finalized at the end of 1971. In Spring 1970, the Institutum Liturgicum of Salzburg published a study edition of the Roman model rite, which retained the possibility of using existing practices, was facultatively introduced by the Austrian bishops' conference, and has also been applied in many dioceses outside Austria as an intermediate solution. The existing draft contains a basic rite with a short service of the word in the cemetery chapel, the burial, and the concluding celebration of the Eucharist—which under certain circumstances can begin with the offertory. A second basic rite includes three celebrations: at the house, in the church (together with a mass), and at the graveside. A series of variations are provided for both rites; there is a special rite for a cremation.

On the reform of the breviary it should be remarked that in 1970 the "New Book of Hours" was passed by the bishops' conferences, and officially approved on 9 November 1970 for fulfilment of the obligation. The permission is to hold until the definitive edition of a German-language breviary appears.

A final regulation concerns the question of vestments, which is generally under discussion today. The guide-lines for celebrations in small groups have already opened up the possibility of a reduction in certain situations. The Austrian liturgical commission made the following recommendation to the bishops' conference at the beginning of 1971: "On account of the minimal progress in this regard there should be no general regulation, and permission in this respect should be at the discretion of the ordinary responsible. The Austrian liturgical commission also recommends that individual bishops permit the already usual practice of new forms of chasuble with a stole worn over them in the colour of the day." The Austrian bishops' conference approved this recommendation. In regard to the calendar, it is proposed to establish a regional calendar for the entire language area.

This short survey of the liturgical legislation for the German-speaking countries shows that the bishops' conferences have managed a considerable amount. They have taken into account their responsibility to the whole Church as well as to existing liturgical legislation, and have paid due regard to existing uses and customs. The fact that every regulation did not meet with universal satisfaction was certainly not the fault solely of an absence of will and concern on the part of the bishops' conferences.

Translated by John Griffiths

Mary Collins

Local Liturgical Legislation: United States of America

AT THIS stage in the renewal of Roman Catholic worship in the United States, ensuring suitable reverence for the Eucharist dominates the range of liturgical concerns of the American bishops. This concern has shown itself in recent disciplinary decisions of the National Conference of Catholic Bishops concerning receiving communion under both kinds and receiving communion in the hand.

The general Roman instruction of June 1970 authorized an extension of the occasions on which it is permissible for worshippers to share the eucharistic cup. In November 1970, the U.S. bishops considered recommendations for national concessions in this matter. After debate they approved four and denied two of the requested extensions. At the discretion of the individual bishop in his diocese, the celebrating priest may now be authorized to share the cup with the faithful in attendance at funeral masses or other special family occasions; on days of special religious or civil significance for the people of the United States (such as Thanksgiving day or Independence day); during Holy Week at the Holy Thursday Eucharist and at the Easter Vigil; and at weekday masses.

The Conference denied the extension of this concession to share the cup with the congregation assembled on Sundays or on holydays of obligation. Among the prominent factors in this restriction was, first, an uncertainty about how to cope with the large number of worshippers, because no adequate rite exists. Further, time pressures were anticipated, particularly in urban areas, should it become customary for these large numbers to receive under both kinds. Since leisure in worship is not a commonly shared value in American Catholicism, the prospect of a lengthened liturgy was not considered pastorally attractive.

The movement towards eucharistic self-communication has gained momentum in many parts of the United States. The Federation of Diocesan Liturgical Commissions, a grass-roots pastoral organization, sponsored informal research indicating the growing acceptance of this custom contrary to existing disciplinary law. Through the influence of the FDLC a proposal to seek authorization from Rome for communion in the hand at the option of the individual communicant was brought to the national bishops' meeting in November 1970. There it was defeated through failure to gain support of two-thirds of the bishops present and voting. It did receive a simple majority of 117 affirmative and 107 negative votes. However, episcopal opposition to communion in the hand in any form has led in some dioceses to explicit prohibition of passing the chalice directly to the communicant, even when the cup is legitimately to be shared.

At the same meeting in which the American bishops rejected self-communication of the eucharistic bread, the episcopal conference approved an alternative liberalization of discipline with regard to eucharistic communion. Bishops, according to their judgment, may name individual lay men and women, as well as religious, in their dioceses whom they wish to authorize to assist the priests in giving communion at masses with large congregations. This authorization may extend also to carrying communion to the sick when an ordained priest is not available for this ministry.

The bishops clearly intend to maintain great reserve in the matter of appropriate forms of eucharistic communion. Their cautious attitude towards the masses of American Catholics and preference for "special concessions" points to the great need for adult eucharistic education at all levels in the American church.

The recent authorization of lay and religious *women* as well as men to distribute communion promises at long last to bring to a formal close the American debate about the appropriateness of women readers in the liturgy and the suitability of their presence in the sanctuary when they perform the service of lector. A statement on the matter made by the bishops' committee on the liturgy reaffirms the position of *Gaudium et Spes* that "every type of discrimination...is to be overcome and eradicated, as contrary to God's intent". Specifically, it itemized "legitimate liturgical usage", namely, that women may assume the ministries of cantor, lector, leader of song, and commentator; that when a woman reads a lesson she should do so from the same ambo or lectern where the other readings are done; and that in all of these ministries a woman's position inside or outside the sanctuary is simply a decision to be made in the light of circumstances and existing spatial arrangements, not a special case to be considered because of sex. Though the formal position is clear, comfort is clearly given to male prejudices, preferences and fears, with the declaration that implementation of this policy is left "to the judgment of the pastor or the priest who presides over the celebration in the light of the culture and mentality of the congregation". The matter of the liturgical service of woman will only be settled at the local level, even after clear directives have been formulated.

Adaptation to the tempo of American life has taken the form of widespread authorization of Saturday eucharistic celebrations anticipating the liturgy of the Sunday. Increasing numbers of parishes schedule Saturday afternoon and evening masses as well as Sunday morning celebrations, to make it more convenient for the faithful "to satisfy the precept of participating in mass". To facilitate the priests' pastoral ministry in this new situation, a priest may trinate on Saturday when wedding or funeral masses are celebrated earlier in the day.

Accommodation to the continued crowds of Catholic worshippers has resulted in episcopal authorization for repeating the solemn liturgy of Good Friday, "if the size or nature of a parish or other community indicates the pastoral need for an additional service". Similarly, on the Saturday of the Easter Vigil, a second mass of the Vigil may be permitted for pastoral reasons—size, convenience of the faithful— after the entire vigil service has once been celebrated in that place.

Intensive concern for the discipline of eucharistic worship has had the consequence that liturgical decisions in other areas have been minimal. Where changes have been made regarding the age proper for children's first confession or for confirmation, these changes have come in individual dioceses. No national directives have been issued either to discourage or encourage new approaches for these sacramental celebrations.

Despite, or because of, the absence of leadership in renewal, interest in developing rites for common absolution after auricular confession continues to grow in the American church. However, the actual conditions of the country regarding adult practice of the sacrament of penance are not known. Official research into the situation, sponsored by the episcopal conference, is a needed precondition for any disciplinary developments in this area. What is more likely to come in the near future is an unofficial survey initiated by the Diocesan Federation of Liturgical Commissions and continued independent research. Only subsequently will the episcopal conference begin to acknowledge and respond to the emerging pastoral problem, if past patterns prevail.

Recent months have shown that the grass-roots Federation of Diocesan Liturgical Commissions, which was formally constituted as recently as 1970, may begin to play an important role in the development of future liturgical discipline. If the Federation succeeds in its present efforts to sponsor developments in the area of liturgical adaptations for groups needing special pastoral care (e.g., retarded children, adolescents), the procedural dilemmas which have impeded progress in liturgical renewal in the United States may be closer to resolution.

Evert de Jong

Liturgical Legislation in the Netherlands

AN attempt to summarize the liturgical legislation in the Netherlands raises the question of the desirability and actuality of such
measures. Since the Second Vatican Council promulgated the
Constitution on the Liturgy a very alive and active situation has
developed in the Netherlands. Many have discovered that rubrics
so often applied juridically do not really seem to be so compul-
sory as was once made out. That this newly achieved freedom
does not appear so salutary to everyone is obvious: the liturgists
are often not used to it.

In general it would seem necessary to mark out two groups.
One of them wants the bishops to have all Roman liturgical
documents and pronouncements translated as literally as possible and—with Rome's approval—made binding. These individuals defend their demand with an appeal to orthodoxy and
Roman instructions. There is often an absence of sufficient knowledge of exactly what the Roman documents say and of an adequate understanding of what liturgy really is. The other group is
more concerned to avoid any strict regulation of matters liturgical. Among the many divergent grounds cited, I should think
the most prominent is that legislation and a detailed rubricization
would obscure the real nature of the cult, and would not help
to establish a bond between liturgy and real life. There has been
a considerable manifestation of creativity within this group which
bears witness to an enrichment of the liturgy. Even then, a better
acquaintance with the details of the Roman documents would
not be out of place.

Active participation—so heavily stressed by the Constitution —has taken a new form in the Netherlands in the formation of many parochial working groups, which were inspired by the diocesan liturgical commissions and, under the guidance of liturgical advisers, are now intensively concerned with a rethinking of liturgy and with the preparation of liturgical services. An attempt is made to discover the essentials of liturgy in order to take them into account even when they do not wholly accord with the central authority of the Church.

These active groups receive encouragement and appropriate action from the bishops. They require "confirmation" of their sincere intentions and not "legislation", which is experienced as non-authentic and contrary to a genuine liturgy. A new liturgical legislation would be conceived rather as a piece of church politics than as an aid and a stimulus to arriving at a dynamic relation with God. For some time now, people have been discovering that too individual a form of expression can affect communication and that a certain alienation of the entire church community can result. Nevertheless, that does not mean that the right course is a literal acceptance of a "universal liturgy" that would bring uniformity and therefore be untrue to life—although such a universalization is the aim of the first-mentioned group.

A policy of church leadership that would allow the utterance of genuinely lived expressions of belief cannot rest upon a uni-literal emphasis on fixed liturgical ideas without injuring the unity of all with the Church. In order to stimulate and work along with this liturgical development the Netherlands liturgical commission (with the approval of the Dutch bishops) made a number of pastoral changes in 1969 regarding the individual sacraments, burial of the dead (cremation), church music, and prayer services. In the following years these measures were revised and extended to such themes as youth liturgies, the family, and a commentary on the *ordo missae*. The administrative responsibility for the liturgy has now been entrusted to the National Liturgical Council, consisting of a vicar from each diocese. This council has decided to make the *Directorium voor de Nederlandse Kerkprovincie* a guide-line for its methods. On the basis of the Roman liturgical documents, explanations and amplifications were offered which took into account practical experience from all over the Dutch church.[1] By treating the Roman documents not as fixed rules but as guide-lines, the council hopes to further communication and to make a contribution to responsible liturgical observance.

To illustrate this tendency, I shall list some of the points which are covered in the Directory. Communion in the hand, which is already a widespread practice, was mentioned and described in the first edition. In the second edition (for 1970) it was reported that the Netherlands episcopate had approved the practice on 18 September 1969. Distribution of communion by the laity appears in the edition for 1972, even though the bishops had already provided for the possibility in an instruction on the liturgy of June 1967. Communion in two kinds is again provided for in the 1971 edition. Under the aspect of the "house liturgy", there was already considerable opportunity for the practice. Regulations for the house liturgy were already provided for in the first edition of the Directory in 1969. The same issue contained the new order of readings. The new calendar has been in use since 1970.

In the matter of the new *ordo missae*, in March 1970, in addition to a translation of this *ordo*, a second, experimental, one was allowed which was more appropriate in practice. At the same time, this second *ordo* has a series of eucharistic prayers selected from more than seventy by the Netherlands liturgical commission. The aid of a considerable number of theologians, exegetes and liturgists was invoked for this purpose by the commission.[2]

With regard to the sacrament of penance, the Directory contains three schemes. One is for private confession (in dialogue with the confessor), a second for communal penance (communal preparation and absolution, separate confession), and a third for the celebration of penitence (without separate confession but with a prayer for forgiveness). In the last case it was stressed that the

---

[1] See the Foreword to the *Directorium voor de Ned. Kerkprovince*, 1972 (obtainable from the secretariat of the Nat. Raad voor Liturgie, Biltstraat 119, Utrecht).

[2] Ned. Comm. v. Lit.: *Missaal, Pt. 1: Ordo Missae* (obtainable from N.V. Gooi en Sticht, Hilversum).

service was without absolution, yet those who use it take absolution as included under "prayer for forgiveness".

It is hoped that with the publication of this Directory every year it will be possible to provide not only the calendar but an account of essential guide-lines, so that information will reach pastors quickly. This will help to give a positive encouragement to a self-developing liturgy.

Translated by John Griffiths